HOWARD BRENTON

Howard Brenton was born in Portsmouth in 1942. His many plays include *Christie in Love* (Portable Theatre, 1969); *Revenge* (Theatre Upstairs, 1969); *Magnificence* (Royal Court Theatre, 1973); *The Churchill Play* (Nottingham Playhouse, 1974, and twice revived by the RSC, 1978 and 1988); *Bloody Poetry* (Foco Novo, 1984, and Royal Court Theatre, 1987); *Weapons of Happiness* (National Theatre, Evening Standard Award, 1976); *Epsom Downs* (Joint Stock Theatre, 1977); *Sore Throats* (RSC, 1978); *The Romans in Britain* (National Theatre, 1980, revived at the Crucible Theatre, Sheffield, 2006); *Thirteenth Night* (RSC, 1981); *The Genius* (1983), *Greenland* (1988) and *Berlin Bertie* (1992), all presented by the Royal Court; *Kit's Play* (RADA Jerwood Theatre, 2000); *Paul* (National Theatre, 2005); *In Extremis* (Shakespeare's Globe, 2006 and 2007); *Never So Good* (National Theatre, 2008); *The Ragged Trousered Philanthropists* adapted from the novel by Robert Tressell (Liverpool Everyman and Chichester Festival Theatre, 2010); *Anne Boleyn* (Shakespeare's Globe, 2010 and 2011); *55 Days* (Hampstead Theatre, 2012); *#aiww: The Arrest of Ai Weiwei* (Hampstead Theatre, 2013) and *The Guffin* (NT Connections, 2013).

Collaborations with other writers include *Brassneck* (with David Hare, Nottingham Playhouse, 1972); *Pravda* (with David Hare, National Theatre, Evening Standard Award, 1985) and *Moscow Gold* (with Tariq Ali, RSC, 1990).

Versions of classics include *The Life of Galileo* (1980) and *Danton's Death* (1982) both for the National Theatre, Goethe's *Faust* (1995/6) for the RSC, a new version of *Danton's Death* for the National Theatre (2010) and *Dances of Death* (Gate Theatre, 2013).

He wrote thirteen episodes of the BBC1 drama series *Spooks* (2001–05, BAFTA Best Drama Series, 2003).

Howard Brenton

DRAWING
THE LINE

NICK HERN BOOKS

London

www.nickhernbooks.co.uk

A Nick Hern Book

Drawing the Line first published in Great Britain as a paperback original in 2013 by Nick Hern Books Limited, The Glasshouse, 49a Goldhawk Road, London W12 8QP, in association with Hampstead Theatre, London

Typeset by Nick Hern Books, London
Printed in the UK by Mimeo Ltd, Huntingdon, Cambridgeshire PE29 6XX

A CIP catalogue record for this book is available from the British Library

ISBN 978 1 84842 372 5

Drawing the Line was first performed at Hampstead Theatre, London, on 3 December 2013, with the following cast:

LORD PETHICK-LAWRENCE/ BRITISH ARMY SERGEANT	David Annen
MUHAMMAD ALI JINNAH	Paul Bazely
CYRIL RADCLIFFE	Tom Beard
LADY EDWINA MOUNTBATTEN	Lucy Black
JAWAHARLAL NEHRU	Silas Carson
ANTONIA RADCLIFFE	Abigail Cruttenden
JUSTICE MEHR CHAND MAHAJAN/ VILLAGER	Neil D'Souza
MOHANDAS GANDHI/ELDER/ JUSTICE TEJA SINGH	Tanveer Ghani
LORD LOUIS MOUNTBATTEN	Andrew Havill
DALIT WOMAN/KALVATI	Salma Hoque
CHAUDHRY MUHAMMAD ALI /AIDE TO NEHRU/INDIAN PHOTOGRAPHER	Rez Kempton
CLEMENT ATLEE	John MacKay
LIAQUAT ALI KHAN/VILLAGER/ AIDE TO NEHRU/JUSTICE DIN MUHAMMAD	Simon Nagra
RAO V.D. AYER/YOUNG MAN	Nikesh Patel
CHRISTOPHER BEAUMONT	Brendan Patricks
DALIT WOMAN/TARAVATI	Shalini Peiris
YOUNG MAN/AIDE TO JINNAH/ LORD KRISHNA	Peter Singh

Director	Howard Davies
Designer	Tim Hatley
Costume Designer	Jack Galloway
Lighting Designer	Rick Fisher
Composer	Nicki Wells
Casting	Suzanne Crowley *and* Gilly Poole
Sound Designer	Mike Walker

Characters

CLEMENT ATLEE
LORD PETHICK-LAWRENCE
CYRIL RADCLIFFE
ANTONIA RADCLIFFE
FIRST VILLAGER
SECOND VILLAGER
VILLAGE ELDER
FIRST YOUNG MAN
CHRISTOPHER BEAUMONT
SECOND YOUNG MAN
FIRST DALIT WOMAN
SECOND DALIT WOMAN
BRITISH ARMY SERGEANT
BRITISH PRIVATE
LORD LOUIS
    MOUNTBATTEN
LADY EDWINA
    MOUNTBATTEN
PHOTOGRAPHER
JAWAHARLAL NEHRU
MOHANDAS GANDHI
TARAVATI
JUSTICE MEHR CHAND
    MAHAJAN
BOY
RAO V.D. AYER

AIDE TO NEHRU
MUHAMMAD ALI JINNAH
LIAQUAT ALI KHAN
ABEER
JUSTICE DIN MUHAMMAD
CHAUDHRY MUHAMMAD
    ALI
JUSTICE TEJA SINGH
LORD KRISHNA
KALAVATI
FIRST WOMAN
SECOND WOMAN

Plus SERVANTS, AIDES

The action takes place during July and August 1947 in London, Delhi and the Punjab.

This text went to press before the end of rehearsals and so may differ slightly from the play as performed.

ACT ONE

Scene One

Prime Minister CLEMENT ATLEE, *sixty-four*, *and the Secretary of State for India* LORD PETHICK-LAWRENCE, *seventy-six*.

CYRIL RADCLIFFE, *forty-eight*, *has just come into the room*.

ATLEE *is smoking a pipe*.

ATLEE. Ah, Cyril.

RADCLIFFE. Good afternoon, Prime Minister.

Handshakes.

ATLEE. How is Mrs Radcliffe?

RADCLIFFE. She is very well, thank you.

ATLEE. Send her my greetings. And my apologies.

RADCLIFFE. Apologies? For what?

ATLEE. We'll see.

Awkward pause. ATLEE *is looking at* RADCLIFFE *thoughtfully*.

PETHICK-LAWRENCE. Er…

ATLEE. Yes, do you know Lord Pethick-Lawrence?

RADCLIFFE. Actually, I've not had the pleasure.

PETHICK-LAWRENCE. Mr Justice Radcliffe.

Handshakes.

ATLEE. Fred here is Secretary of State for India.

RADCLIFFE. So I do believe.

PETHICK-LAWRENCE. For my sins.

He smiles. RADCLIFFE *finds their timing impossible to read.*

ATLEE. Interesting day in court, Cyril?

RADCLIFFE. A crook, trying it on.

ATLEE. Alarming number do, these days.

RADCLIFFE. There are rotten apples.

ATLEE. It's part of the British genius, fiddling on the side in times of austerity.

RADCLIFFE. Oh, despite what I see in my court, I think as a nation we're better than that.

ATLEE. Do you now.

RADCLIFFE. On the whole, decency holds firm.

Another awkward pause.

ATLEE. Up for something more challenging? Rather than sending down the odd, indecently rotten apple?

RADCLIFFE. Well, yes, of course, delighted to serve in any way I can. If it be in my power.

ATLEE. Mm. (*Pipe puff.*) Do you know it?

RADCLIFFE. Know what?

ATLEE. India.

RADCLIFFE. No, Prime Minister…

ATLEE. Never been?

RADCLIFFE. No.

ATLEE. Excellent.

RADCLIFFE. Why?

A pause.

ATLEE. Fred?

PETHICK-LAWRENCE. We want you to draw a line.

RADCLIFFE (*aside*). And I've said yes. Yes. Out of the blue yonder I've just heard myself say: 'Yes. Of course, Prime Minister.' And I think I heard myself say: 'It's an honour.'

Exit ATLEE *and* PETHICK-LAWRENCE.

RADCLIFFE *remains on stage.*

Scene Two

Enter ANTONIA RADCLIFFE, *forty-four.*

RADCLIFFE. I just heard myself say 'yes'.

ANTONIA. On the spot?

RADCLIFFE. On the spot.

ANTONIA. On the spot in Downing Street! It's a great honour, Cyril.

RADCLIFFE. Yes.

ANTONIA. Tiny little problem, though. You know bugger all about India!

RADCLIFFE. Absolutely squelch!

They laugh.

Though that's the reason why they've asked me. Atlee says the Government want a fresh eye.

ANTONIA. Oh, Cyril, it will be a wonder. The beginning of an honourable end to Empire.

RADCLIFFE. It has to come. A new world.

ANTONIA. You are perfect for it.

RADCLIFFE. Well, I can try to offer a rational overview.

ANTONIA. To cut through.

RADCLIFFE. Gordian knot, yes. I'll be briefed intensively of course, the Viceroy's putting together a team for me.

ANTONIA. Well, thank God you're a fast learner.

RADCLIFFE. That the law has given me.

They are looking at each other, very excited.

ANTONIA. Million and one things... where will you stay?

RADCLIFFE. Delhi, of course. Viceroy House.

ANTONIA. With the Mountbattens?

RADCLIFFE. Yes.

ANTONIA. Sorry, mind spinning. God. Kiss me.

They kiss.

So how long...

RADCLIFFE. Five weeks.

ANTONIA. Five weeks before you go, well, that gives some time... order clothes for the heat and...

RADCLIFFE. No, I have to do the job in five weeks.

A pause.

ANTONIA. That's...

RADCLIFFE. It's a challenge. I'll finish the case I'm sitting tomorrow, then the next day... (*Aeroplane gesture.*) Off to Delhi!

ANTONIA. It's impossible. You'll have to see something of the country, and the negotiations...

RADCLIFFE. That's the timetable. Atlee wants the India Independence Act through Parliament in two weeks' time. It will set the date for independence as August fifteenth. That means the border must be settled a week earlier. Five weeks!

ANTONIA. They can't ask this of you.

RADCLIFFE. It has to be quick and decisive. They don't want '42 all over again.

ANTONIA. '42?

RADCLIFFE. The anti-British riots.

ANTONIA. Dear God, one forgets. It's all so far away.

RADCLIFFE. I want you to come out with me.

ANTONIA. You try and stop me!

RADCLIFFE. Leave it a fortnight then…

ANTONIA. Yes, that would be wonderful. Staying at Viceroy House.

RADCLIFFE. Yes.

ANTONIA. Oh, Cyril, this could lead to…

RADCLIFFE. Yes, I know.

ANTONIA. I'll go and think about packing. Will you need shorts?

RADCLIFFE. God, I hope not.

ANTONIA. If I've two weeks, I'll try to buy something for me.

RADCLIFEE. You'll look wonderful.

Peck of a cheek. She exits.

(*Aside*.) Right. (*A pause*.) Right. Steady the buffs. There is that drive, secretly, always: that you may even personally be remembered for something good, even great, or going on for great. What was it Leonardo said: 'To live on in the minds of men'? Better not owned up to, of course, not in England. But with the advantage I have in life, to give something back, that would be very fine. To make a splash in the world.

He exits.

Scene Three

Light and heat.

A village in the Punjab.

A small café. Worn upright chairs. A small table. A portrait of Jinnah.

A group of VILLAGE MEN *sit drinking tea. A* VILLAGE ELDER, *two others and a thin* YOUNG MAN *who has a walking stick.*

Nothing happens for a while. Tea is drunk.

Then enter CHRISTOPHER BEAUMONT, *thirty-five. He has rather long fair hair, he is dressed in Indian clothes, there is a T.E. Lawrence dash about him. He carries saddlebags.*

FIRST VILLAGER (*Punjabi*). *Hai Rabba ai ki jegg haigi?*

SECOND VILLAGER (*Punjabi*). *Angrej lagda he.*

FIRST VILLAGER (*Punjabi*). *Jithe vi jao chitte chuhe milde nen.*

　　They laugh, though the YOUNG MAN *does not.*

　　(*Aside.*) I said: 'Dear God what is that thing?'

SECOND VILLAGER (*aside*). I said: 'It must be English.'

FIRST VILLAGER (*aside*). I said: 'White mice everywhere.'

　　They laugh again. A SECOND YOUNG MAN – *teens – runs on.* CHRISTOPHER *gives him some coins. The* SECOND YOUNG MAN *runs off.*

　　CHRISTOPHER *approaches them.*

CHRISTOPHER. Salaam.

　　They hesitate. Then the ELDER *resolves the moment by taking* CHRISTOPHER's *hand.*

ELDER. As-Salaam Alaikum.

The other two MEN *also shake hands. The* YOUNG MAN does not.

The ELDER*'s English is accented but good.*

CHRISTOPHER. My horse...

ELDER. The boy will attend to her. Please, drink some tea.

CHRISTOPHER. That is very civil of you.

CHRISTOPHER *sits.*

ELDER. Sir, why ride a horse?

CHRISTOPHER. It's a good way to see the country.

ELDER. You can't see it from a car?

CHRISTOPHER. Yes, but on horseback one gets a personal perspective.

Incomprehension.

CHRISTOPHER *takes out a cigarette case and offers cigarettes to the* MEN*, who accept with the exception of the* FIRST YOUNG MAN.

The ELDER *takes out a box of matches and lights the cigarettes all round.*

Polite smiles as they smoke.

Unnoticed by the smokers, two DALIT *('untouchable')* WOMEN *enter. They are poorly dressed. They have old baskets tied to their backs. They stare at the smoking men.*

FIRST WOMAN (*Punjabi*). *Ai ki jegg haigi?*

SECOND WOMAN (*Punjabi*). *Angrez lagda hai.*

FIRST WOMAN (*Punjabi*). *Hari sanu bacha lao.*

They laugh.

(*Aside.*) I said: 'What is that?'

SECOND WOMAN (*aside*). I said: 'It must be English.'

FIRST WOMAN (*aside*). And I said: 'The Lord Krishna preserve us.'

They laugh again and exit.

CHRISTOPHER *notices a small military badge pinned to the* ELDER's *lapel.*

CHRISTOPHER. Your badge. You served in the Red Eagle Division?

ELDER. 4th Indian Infantry, yes, sir.

CHRISTOPHER. Against the Italians in the Sudan?

ELDER. Yes. And then in Syria.

CHRISTOPHER. Distinguished service.

The ELDER *does not respond.*

A pause while tea is poured. Nods and smiles.

Gentlemen. What I'm doing is travelling through the Punjab, to test reaction on the ground.

They do not know what he is talking about.

Reaction to the British Commission?

ELDER. What Commission?

CHRISTOPHER. The Commission to draw the line.

ELDER. What line?

CHRISTOPHER. The border.

ELDER. There is to be a border?

CHRISTOPHER. Yes, between India and Pakistan.

The ELDER *stares at him.*

ELDER. There is no Pakistan.

CHRISTOPHER. The Government in London are sending a Commission… a committee… to draw the map of Pakistan.

ELDER. Pakistan is in my heart but where is it on Earth?

CHRISTOPHER. The British are going to decide where it is.

The ELDER *stares at him for a moment.*

ELDER. In the Army, we were the soldiers, Hindu, Muslim, Sikh, but the officers were British.

CHRISTOPHER. I'm sorry, sir, I don't...

FIRST YOUNG MAN. He means, if there is to be a Pakistan, it is in the eye of God. And not in the gift of the British.

CHRISTOPHER. Unfortunately, it is in our gift. Would that it were not, but...

FIRST YOUNG MAN. If we want a Pakistan we will take it from you.

He knocks his chair flying.

ELDER (*Punjabi*). *Muhammed maafi mung!*

But the FIRST YOUNG MAN *exits.*

Forgive my nephew. He was injured in the riots in Calcutta last year. His brother was killed. I think you are an honourable man, sir. So I tell you... (*Lowers his voice.*) I am giving him shelter.

CHRISTOPHER. I understand.

ELDER. In the end it's the little things.

CHRISTOPHER. Little...

ELDER. See!

He holds up the box of matches. The other two MEN *are at once alert.*

CHRISTOPHER. Matches?

FIRST MAN (*Urdu*). *Ye baniye jan ke qimat berhate hain!*

CHRISTOPHER. The Baniye...?

ELDER. The Hindus. He says they force up the prices.

CHRISTOPHER. Of matches...

SECOND MAN (*Urdu*). *Aur kafan ki qimat.*

ELDER. And they force up the price of kafans.

CHRISTOPHER. Kafans? Funeral shrouds?

ELDER. They control the cloth, they force up the price.

CHRISTOPHER. I'm sure these are rumours…

ELDER. No. It's the little things.

The FIRST YOUNG MAN *enters, running.*

FIRST YOUNG MAN. British Army! British Army!

ELDER (*to* CHRISTOPHER). The little things kill.

The FIRST YOUNG MAN *exits, running.*

A BRITISH ARMY SERGEANT *and a* BRITISH PRIVATE *enter. The* PRIVATE *has a rifle in his hands.*

CHRISTOPHER *stands.*

The VILLAGE MEN *stand and step back.*

SERGEANT. Mr Christopher Beaumont, sir?

CHRISTOPHER. Yes, yes, Sergeant. (*To the* ELDER.) Will you please excuse me for a moment?

ELDER. You came with him?

CHRISTOPHER. No, no, I'm travelling independently…

ELDER. You came with the Army?

CHRISTOPHER. No, no…

ELDER. You have brought the Army to the village?

SERGEANT. Been all over the shop looking for you, sir.

CHRISTOPHER. Why, what…

SERGEANT. Urgent telegram for you from Delhi.

FIRST VILLAGER (*Punjabi*). *Hareq carsi ehe cheeji karde hun.*

SECOND VILLAGER (*Punjabi*). *British, nu tusi kadi jakeen karsakde!*

CHRISTOPHER. Good God, man, coming after me out here, bit extreme…

SERGEANT. Aim to please, sir.

But he is nervous.

CHRISTOPHER *opens the telegram and reads it as the two* VILLAGERS *back away…*

ELDER. Sir… leave now.

CHRISTOPHER (*does not hear him. Reads the telegram*). Who the Hell is Cyril Radcliffe?

ELDER. Go! The Hindus will have seen us talking to Army…

The SECOND YOUNG MAN *runs on and throws a stone at the* SERGEANT, *who draws a pistol, as…*

SERGEANT. Sir! The jeep!

ELDER. It has all gone too far, you see. Too far.

He turns, pulling the FIRST YOUNG MAN *around.*

CHRISTOPHER. Too far? I pray not so…

ELDER (*Punjabi*). *Paran hat!*

Stones fly.

The PRIVATE *fires his rifle.*

More stones.

SERGEANT. Sir! To the jeep! Now!

CHRISTOPHER. But my horse… (*A stone hits his hand.*) Ah!

SERGEANT. For God's sake, man, get in the jeep!

They exit, running.

The shouts and screams die down.

Enter two DALIT WOMEN. *They move with a slow, steady exhaustion. They have baskets on their backs. They pick up the stones, throwing them over their shoulders into the baskets. They come to the cigarette stubs left by the overturned table and chairs. They sniff at them, pick them up and put them in their pockets.*

FIRST WOMAN (*aside*). You can make a little bit of money out of anything.

SECOND WOMAN (*aside*). Even if it's a riot.

FIRST WOMAN (*aside*). Even if it's the country tearing itself apart.

They laugh and exit.

Scene Four

Viceroy House. Imperial splendour: mirrors, gold stucco.

LORD MOUNTBATTEN, *forty-seven, is in white dress uniform.*

LADY EDWINA MOUNTBATTEN, *forty-six, is in a beautiful, shimmering evening dress. She stands to one side, smiling.*

MOUNTBATTEN *stands with* CYRIL RADCLIFFE, *who is in a dark suit.*

An Indian PHOTOGRAPHER *with flash equipment is about to photograph* MOUNTBATTEN *and* RADCLIFFE.

Two Indian SERVANTS, *immaculately dressed, white gloves, at a distance.*

MOUNTBATTEN. Radcliffe, come. Can you see the back of our heads in this damn mirror?

PHOTOGRAPHER. I think it's all right, sir.

MOUNTBATTEN (*to the* PHOTOGRAPHER). Could you possibly just take it over here? There's a bit of thin, I'm afraid. A bald patch? Not exactly the Imperial impression one should pass off. Radcliffe, come.

They move.

That's it. And Edwina, you too.

EDWINA. Isn't this meant to be a rather official photograph, darling?

MOUNTBATTEN. Oh, damn official. Half-turn. Always know one's best side. Ha!

RADCLIFFE *feels awkward*.

The PHOTOGRAPHER *prepares*.

If you are suffering from the flight there are things in India called essential oils. Edwina's very keen, you can set him to rights, can't you, darling?

EDWINA. Be delighted.

RADCLIFFE. I really am all right, sir.

PHOTOGRAPHER. Excuse me, Your Excellency, I am ready.

MOUNTBATTEN. Jolly good. I don't think we should say 'cheese'. Noël Coward told me that when being photographed one should say 'lesbian nuns'.

EDWINA (*laughs*). Oh, Dicky, do stop it.

MOUNTBATTEN. Yes, moment of gravitas. Let's say 'Lord's Cricket Ground'. Ready?

They pose.

One… two… three.

Then in unison – RADCLIFFE *mumbling*.

MOUNTBATTEN/EDWINA/RADCLIFFE. Lord's Cricket Ground.

The photograph is taken. The MOUNTBATTENS *laugh*.

MOUNTBATTEN (*to the* PHOTOGRAPHER). Thank you so much.

PHOTOGRAPHER. Delighted to be of service, Viceroy.

MOUNTBATTEN. Yes yes, very good.

He looks at EDWINA.

Enter CHRISTOPHER.

The PHOTOGRAPHER *exits as the scene continues*.

EDWINA. Oh, Mr Beaumont. I do hope you're well after your latest escapade?

CHRISTOPHER. I am perfectly well, thank you.

MOUNTBATTEN. Mr Radcliffe. This is Mr Christopher Beaumont, who is to be your Secretary on the Commission.

RADCLIFFE. Very pleased to meet you, Mr Beaumont. I'm delighted you are going to help.

CHRISTOPHER. It's a privilege, sir.

EDWINA. Christopher, the feeling in the Punjab villages, is there any hope of stopping it?

CHRISTOPHER *about to reply…*

MOUNTBATTEN. Edwina, we must get on.

EDWINA. Of course. Gentlemen, please excuse me.

CHRISTOPHER. My Lady.

RADCLIFFE. My Lady.

She smiles again and goes but lurks to overhear.

MOUNTBATTEN. So, Radcliffe. All you need, you will have.

RADCLIFFE. Thank you, sir, I…

MOUNTBATTEN. I'm putting you in the bungalow. It's within the grounds of Viceroy House, so it's secure.

RADCLIFFE. Thank you, sir.

MOUNTBATTEN. Financial side sorted and stowed? Your fee and such…?

RADCLIFFE. Yes, sir.

MOUNTBATTEN. Good. And congratulations on the knighthood.

RADCLIFFE. I think that may be rather premature…

MOUNTBATTEN. It is a certainty. Didn't Downing Street give you an indication of the touch of the Royal breadknife?

RADCLIFFE. There was a nod.

MOUNTBATTEN. It will be richly deserved. (*Smiles.*) Well, Mr Justice. You are about to render a great service to the peoples of India and to the Empire. So I think I should leave you to bunk down and get on with it!

RADCLIFFE. There is just one thing, Viceroy.

MOUNTBATTEN. Oh yes?

RADCLIFFE. I very much want to meet Mahatma Gandhi. Go to the fountainhead, get a feel for the culture.

A moment.

MOUNTBATTEN. Virginity.

RADCLIFFE. Viceroy?

MOUNTBATTEN. Keep your virginity, Radcliffe. Don't flirt with things Indian. Too many come out and get thoroughly rogered by this country's culture. That is my very serious advice.

RADCLIFFE. Thank you, Viceroy.

MOUNTBATTEN. Be under no illusion, this will be a bloody business. All we can do is hope to keep an acceptable level of violence.

RADCLIFFE. What level would that be, sir?

MOUNTBATTEN. A hundred thousand deaths?

RADCLIFFE. A hundred thousand…

MOUNTBATTEN. Never breathe you heard me say that. (*A moment.*) Well, there we are. If creature comforts are not up to it down in the bungalow, Beaumont here will see to things through my office. And one last thing, Radcliffe. The Commission is entirely independent. I cannot give you advice, nor will I attempt to influence your decisions in any way. I must keep the Viceroy independent. I think of myself as a flagpole. My job is to just stand here until the Union Jack is run down me. If you see what I mean. Well. That's it. Good luck.

Smiles all round and MOUNTBATTEN *exits.*

CHRISTOPHER. So… you don't know India, sir.

RADCLIFFE. Not at all.

CHRISTOPHER. Asia?

RADCLIFFE. Nowhere near. Used to go to Venice before the war.

CHRISTOPHER. Venice.

They look at each other.

RADCLIFFE. For the churches. You think it's rather rum, don't you, me being given this job?

CHRISTOPHER. Well, sir, presumably you have some interest in maps...

RADCLIFFE. None at all. But don't we have a sense of the overview built into us, isn't that part of being British? That's our education, our heritage, that's how we've run an Empire. Which we will now proceed to dismantle... (*Smiles.*) Divine mapmakers that we are.

CHRISTOPHER. Idealistic, sir.

RADCLIFFE. There is a right way and a wrong way, always, in everything. (*A beat.*) A hundred thousand dead. Do you agree with that figure?

CHRISTOPHER. I fear it could be much greater.

RADCLIFFE. We mustn't let that happen.

CHRISTOPHER. It's... No, of course not.

RADCLIFFE. Do everything we can to ensure that that does not happen. (*A beat.*) Well! To the delights of this bungalow!

CHRISTOPHER. Yes.

They move away.

EDWINA *is still on the stage. She approaches them.*

EDWINA. Could I, for a moment...?

RADCLIFFE. Of course, My Lady...

She glances at CHRISTOPHER *who steps back so as not to hear.*

She takes RADCLIFFE*'s hand.*

EDWINA. Mr Radcliffe, I know my husband has to be neutral but… could I urge to you to speak to Pandit-ji?

RADCLIFFE. To…

EDWINA. To Pandit Nehru.

RADCLIFFE. I will, of course, consult all the leaders…

EDWINA. Yes, but Pandit-ji is here in Viceroy House at the moment, on official business, if you wanted…

RADCLIFFE. Thank you so much, My Lady, but I'm sure you understand I must make my own plans…

EDWINA (*lowers her voice*). Mr Radcliffe, the hope is with Pandit Nehru. Not with the Muslim League. The Viceroy can't say that but I want you to know it.

RADCLIFFE. I…

EDWINA. Don't cut out the heart of India: Calcutta, Lahore, Ferozepur.

She stares at him earnestly. He has no idea what she is talking about. She holds his hand for a while, looking into his eyes.

Then she turns and exits quickly.

RADCLIFFE *rejoins* CHRISTOPHER *and they walk away.*

CHRISTOPHER. Do you mind if I ask you what Lady Mountbatten said to you?

RADCLIFFE. Mentioned a place called Ferozepur? What is that?

CHRISTOPHER. I… will brief you, sir.

RADCLIFFE. She also wanted me to see Nehru right away, said he was in the building.

CHRISTOPHER. Ah.

RADCLIFFE. What?

CHRISTOPHER. Nothing, sir.

They exit.

Scene Five

A corridor in Viceroy House.

LADY MOUNTBATTEN, *anxious. She lights a cigarette.*

A distance away, NEHRU *passes, with two* AIDES *carrying papers, in conversation.*

LADY MOUNTBATTEN *raises her hand to attract his attention. He sees her, says something to the* AIDES *who exit. He hurries down to talk to her, looking around furtively.*

NEHRU. Edwina, we can't...

EDWINA. Shut up.

She strides away, he follows, looking around.

A private place. A pillar.

NEHRU. This is unseemly.

EDWINA. But lovely.

NEHRU. Oh God.

He laughs. They hold each other.

Is this the corridor with the broom cupboard...

EDWINA. Jawaharlal, listen. I've talked to this judge.

NEHRU. And?

EDWINA. Bloody stuffed shirt.

NEHRU. Is he bright?

EDWINA. Oh, bright, but... Darling, he knows nothing of India.

NEHRU. Amateur map-reader then? A keen walker? What is the British mania for walking everywhere...

EDWINA. He knows nothing of maps.

A beat.

NEHRU. Knows nothing of the country, nothing of maps. What is Atlee thinking of?

EDWINA. Judge Cyril Radcliffe is an assassin. Sent to murder our country.

NEHRU. 'Our country'? You really do think of India as your country, don't you.

EDWINA. I've fallen in love with you and you are India.

NEHRU. No no no, Edwina, you must not talk like that, no one 'is' India…

EDWINA. You are, when you're in my bed.

NEHRU. Or in your broom cupboard? Which door was it…

EDWINA. Listen! Dicky's given him Christopher Beaumont as an adviser. He's one of those bloody intellectuals, pro-Islam, fancies he's Lawrence of Arabia. Probably dresses up as an Arab in secret: towel on his head, djellaba, no underwear, you know the kind of thing.

NEHRU. Yes, I know Beaumont.

EDWINA. Radcliffe wants to meet Gandhi. Arrange it. Let this judge feel something of the real India.

NEHRU. 'The real India…'

    NEHRU *scoffs and looks away.*

EDWINA. What have I said?

    He shakes his head.

    Am I of any help to you at all?

NEHRU. You are wonderful.

EDWINA. Don't smarm, Jawaharlal. I can't stand it when you smarm.

NEHRU (*smiles*). I am a politician.

EDWINA. Don't you see it's all…

NEHRU. What?

EDWINA. Nothing.

NEHRU. My dear...

EDWINA. Do you and I know what we're doing?

NEHRU. No, of course we don't.

EDWINA. But it's coming to an end, isn't it.

NEHRU. I suspect love for us will never end.

EDWINA. Smarm.

NEHRU. Second door?

They look at each other, hold hands and exit, running.

Scene Six

MOHANDAS GANDHI*'s house.*

The famous spinning wheel is against a wall.

GANDHI *is sitting on cushions, cross-legged, naked to the waist.*

A young woman, TARAVATI, *sits leaning against him.*

NEHRU *enters.*

TARAVATI *exits quickly, with a smile to* NEHRU.

GANDHI *rises gracefully and extends his arms to* NEHRU.

GANDHI. Namaste, Jarawahal.

NEHRU. Namaste, Gandhi-ji.

They embrace. GANDHI *gestures to* NEHRU *to sit and they do.*

GANDHI. Can I offer you some refreshment?

NEHRU. No no.

GANDHI. Some goats' milk?

NEHRU. I am fine.

GANDHI. Some yogurt, from the goats' milk?

NEHRU. Ah. Yes. Yes that would be most welcome.

GANDHI (*calls out*). Taravati, my dear?

    TARAVATI *enters*.

TARAVATI. Yes, Bapu?

GANDHI. Some of the morning's yogurt for our guest.

TARAVATI. Yes, of course.

    She exits.

GANDHI. She is from Kashmir. Her family sent her to Delhi to be safe.

NEHRU. Like so many.

GANDHI. Yes. She is very warm. I need warmth at nights.

NEHRU. Who does not?

GANDHI. Warmth. Without sexual intercourse.

NEHRU. Of course.

    TARAVATI *enters with a small tray, on it an earthenware mug. She hands it to* NEHRU.

GANDHI. Thank you, my dear.

    She makes a slight curtsey and exits.

NEHRU. You are not...

GANDHI. I am fasting today.

NEHRU. Ah.

    He does not want the yogurt but sips.

    Well, Bapu...

GANDHI. Well, Jawaharlal. A British judge come to rip India apart like an old cloth.

NEHRU (*smiles*). A colourful way of putting it but perhaps... not helpful?

GANDHI. No? Has he hanged people? The English have a
great tradition of hanging judges. In England and in India:
remember Ferozepur in 1931.

NEHRU. How could we ever forget? But this judge has a liberal
reputation.

GANDHI. Liberal or not, he will want to hang us all.

NEHRU. Not necessarily.

GANDHI. It pains me that you and I so profoundly disagree.
But I cannot support the partition of our country.

NEHRU. Gandhi-ji, you and I in the Congress Party, Jinnah in
the Muslim League, all of us, we 'leaders'... we have lost
control. Fanatics on both sides are running riot, every dawn
there are more dead, on city streets, the country roads... the
bodies of men, women and children in the morning sun,
Hindu and Muslim. Surely our duty is clear: we must regain
our authority.

GANDHI. How? By accepting a border imposed by the British?

NEHRU. There may be no other solution.

GANDHI. There is always another solution.

NEHRU. In God's name, what?

GANDHI. We live together.

GANDHI *smiles*.

NEHRU. Bapu, I fear this judge's ignorance. I implore you, talk
to him, enlighten him.

GANDHI. No.

NEHRU. He could make terrible mistakes, we must negotiate.

GANDHI. No. I will not compromise with the British,
suddenly, after all these years of struggle. They remain the
imperialists, the occupiers of my country.

NEHRU. I say this with a heavy heart. But you are in danger of
making yourself an irrelevance.

GANDHI. If it is God's wish, then I will be irrelevant.

NEHRU. Meet Radcliffe, help him make a just border.

GANDHI. There can be no just border.

NEHRU. There is going to be one anyway!

GANDHI. That does not make it right.

NEHRU. But we will have an India, free, independent,
democratic, tolerant of all faiths. That is what we have
struggled for.

GANDHI. But cut in two. I will not support partition. Vivisect
me, before you vivisect India.

A silence.

Both try to remain calm.

NEHRU. If no border is agreed, what do you think will happen?

GANDHI. After the killings last year, in Calcutta, I toured
Bengal.

NEHRU *is irritated.*

NEHRU. I know.

GANDHI. I prayed, I spoke, I begged for peace.

NEHRU. Yes…

GANDHI. And all heard me. Muslim crowds, Hindi, Christian,
Sikh, Farsi, Jains… all together, raising their voices to
Heaven.

NEHRU. And when you left, did the killings stop?

They did not.

GANDHI. Peace must be possible between all the peoples of
India. In one country.

NEHRU. No, Gandhi-ji. Perhaps we could have had one united,
free country ten years ago, before the war. When Jinnah still
believed in one India, before the British locked the
leadership of both sides up and our extremists made hay.
Before the Muslim League was powerful, before the Hindu
nationalists began walking round in Nazi uniforms, calling

for the death of Muslims. But not now. It has gone too far, the hatred, the killing. Too far. The only hope is for two countries that can live with each other.

GANDHI. I will fast for peace, I will pray.

NEHRU. Bapu, I fear that will not be enough. In remembrance of all we have struggled for, help me…

He embraces GANDHI, *who strokes his arm affectionately.*

GANDHI. Hush hush, Jawaharlal, I will always love you. But you will have to bear this burden as best you can.

NEHRU. You are deserting our people.

GANDHI. No, I am joining them.

NEHRU. Then so be it.

NEHRU *stands abruptly.*

GANDHI. I seek the less harmful path.

NEHRU. You think I don't?

GANDHI. I think you seek a victory.

NEHRU. I do. The victory of democracy in India.

GANDHI. In all of India?

They look at each other. Then NEHRU *turns away and leaves. He stays on the stage.*

TARAVATI *enters.*

A pause, GANDHI *very still.*

I never weep. In all the years, I never have. Will you weep for me?

TARAVATI *goes to* GANDHI *and embraces him.*

Scene Seven

NEHRU *alone on the stage.*

NEHRU (*aside*). Life is like a game of cards. The hand you are
dealt is determinism; the way you play it is free will.

A tea party in the garden of NEHRU*'s house is assembled
around him. Very English garden tables, Indian awnings.*

A man – grey beard – sits a distance away. He is JUSTICE
MEHR CHAND MAHAJAN. *A* BOY *holds an umbrella
over his head.*

NEHRU *goes and talks to* MAHAJAN.

Mehr, we are agreed, yes?

MAHAJAN. Yes, Pandit-ji.

NEHRU. Play dumb.

MAHAJAN. Tactics.

NEHRU. Yes!

MAHAJAN. Wool over the eyes.

They smile.

NEHRU. You will know the moment to attack. The prize is
great.

MAHAJAN. Kashmir.

NEHRU. No less.

MAHAJAN. Kashmir, always in my heart.

They bow to each other.

NEHRU *walks away.*

Enter RAO V. D. AYER – *late twenties, well groomed,
Oxbridge English.*

RAO. Is tea satisfactory? I sent for scones. There's strawberry jam but no clotted Cornish.

NEHRU. You disapprove? You think we should give him Indian sweets?

RAO. I...

NEHRU. And if we serve him jalebi not scones, do you think the border will go north... ten miles? One mile? One yard?

RAO. Forgive me, Pandit-ji.

NEHRU. You are angry. We are all angry. But we must not let our frustrations, our fury fixate on small things. That is how negotiations failed last year.

RAO. I cannot see how...

NEHRU *stares at him*.

...I can't see how there can be negotiations, with the line to be drawn in five weeks, or, from now, four weeks five days...

NEHRU. Oh, there will be negotiations. And we have the whip hand.

RAO. How...?

NEHRU. Because we are the chaos they fear.

An AIDE *enters*.

RAO. But...

AIDE. Pandit-ji, they are here.

NEHRU. Thank you, show them out here to the garden.

The AIDE *exits*.

Rao, I believe you know Christopher Beaumont?

RAO. Beaumont? Yes, of course.

NEHRU. At Stowe together, weren't you? Then Oxford?

RAO. Yes.

NEHRU. Could you work with him?

RAO. Work…

NEHRU. On Radcliffe's Commission?

RAO. Well…

NEHRU. You are working with him. I've persuaded Viceroy
House to make you Beaumont's assistant.

RAO. I would prefer not…

NEHRU. I need someone close to Radcliffe. You are he.

RAO. But I have strong ideological objections to the
Commission…

NEHRU. Swallow them.

Enter RADCLIFFE, CHRISTOPHER, AIDES o*f the
Commission and of* NEHRU.

RADCLIFFE (*to* CHRISTOPHER). How do I…?

CHRISTOPHER (*to* RADCLIFFE). Mr General Secretary.
Later, Pandit-ji.

NEHRU. Mr Chief Justice, I am delighted to greet you, both
personally in my home and as General Secretary of the India
Congress.

RADCLIFFE. Mr General Secretary, I, too, am delighted to
have this opportunity to meet so quickly. I have a difficult
task in your country.

NEHRU. It will be achieved, given good will.

RADCLIFFE. I assure you.

A moment's awkwardness.

This is Mr Christopher Beaumont.

NEHRU. Pleased to meet you, Mr Beaumont. And, Mr Justice,
this is Mr Rao V.D. Ayer.

RADCLIFFE. Pleased to meet you, Mr Ayer. I understand
Viceroy House has asked you to help?

RAO. Yes.

NEHRU. He is one of the brightest and the best, you have stolen him…

Smiles.

CHRISTOPHER. I'm sorry, I don't…

RADCLIFFE. Yes, I had a phone call from the Viceroy, Mr Ayer will be your assistant.

CHRISTOPHER. I see. (*A moment.*) How are you, Rao?

RAO. Very well, Christopher.

NEHRU. Oh, you know each other?

CHRISTOPHER. Yes.

RADCLIFFE. Well, that's excellent.

NEHRU. And please permit me to introduce the adviser the Congress Party have nominated to your commission.

MAHAJAN *stands. He bows slightly.*

Mr Justice Mehr Chand Mahajan. Mr Justice.

MAHAJAN. Namaste.

RADCLIFFE. I'm very pleased to meet you, Mr Justice.

MAHAJAN (*thick accent*). It will be pleasant to work with so eminent a person as yourself, sir.

RADCLIFFE. Thank you… and indeed likewise.

MAHAJAN. With your permission, I will leave you now. As a formal adviser to the Commission I do not think it correct to socialise.

RADCLIFFE. No, indeed, absolutely.

MAHAJAN. I look forward to our formal discussions.

RADCLIFFE. Yes.

Formal bows.

MAHAJAN *exits with the* BOY *holding up the umbrella.*

NEHRU. So! Teatime!

They sit at the table.

An AIDE *pours tea.*

Mr Beaumont, you were in the Punjab recently, near Ferozepur? On horseback? And you lost the horse?

(*Indicates* CHRISTOPHER*'s bandaged hand.*) You were hurt?

CHRISTOPHER. Not seriously, thank you, sir. Though I do feel responsible.

NEHRU. For the deaths in the riot that followed your visit?

A sticky moment. CHRISTOPHER *tries to find something to say...*

Do not feel so, Mr Beaumont. No doubt you went with good intentions?

CHRISTOPHER. They were not enough.

NEHRU. But they have to be, all our intentions, together they must be good enough. Gentlemen, please, tea.

They sit at the tables. AIDES *pour tea and move about them. Then...*

Mr Justice, I hope you don't think this impertinent, but what did you do during the war?

RADCLIFFE. I was in the Ministry of Information.

NEHRU. And what did that entail?

RADCLIFFE. Telling the public things they needed to know in wartime.

NEHRU. For example?

RADCLIFFE. Oh, how how to make custard without fresh eggs?

NEHRU. And was this achieved with the famous British dried-egg powder?

RADCLIFFE. Yes.

NEHRU. And did the powder have anything to do with eggs?

RADCLIFFE. That was classified information.

Laughter.

And, Pandit-ji, what did you do in the war?

A still, bad moment.

NEHRU. A great deal of reading, since I was in prison.

RADCLIFFE. Of course. Forgive me.

NEHRU. My dear Radcliffe, there have been adverse comments in the press about your, shall we say, innocence of India...

RADCLIFFE.... Yes, of which I am all too painfully aware...

NEHRU. No no, my dear fellow, my point is I welcome your impartiality.

RADCLIFFE. Thank you. And I assure you, I'm not wholly ignorant of the history of my country and yours. The massacre at Amritsar. The hangings at Ferozepur. The British Army's attacks on demonstrators during the salt-tax protest. These are blots on my country's reputation.

A silence.

NEHRU. Blots.

RADCLIFFE. Forgive me if I express myself inappropriately...

NEHRU. No no, my dear fellow. The problem we all have is that, once blood is spilt, disputes between peoples, nations, religions become all but impossible to solve. But we have to act, somehow. It is a hard lesson: 'Drive your cart and plough over the bones of the dead.'

RADCLIFFE. William Blake.

NEHRU. Indeed. Scone?

RADCLIFFE, CHRISTOPHER *and* RAO *stand and walk away.*

(*Aside.*) Oh yes, I can quote their poets at them, serve them tea and scones. I smile and swallow my nausea at their crass, casual ignorance, the massive cruelty of their occupation of my country. But every minute, every second, day and night I work, with every fibre of my being, to get them out. (*A beat.*) How extraordinary it is... that *she* understands that.

NEHRU, AIDES *and tea party exit.*

RAO (*behind* RADCLIFFE). I did not want this.

CHRISTOPHER. We must talk.

RADCLIFFE (*to them both*). Why does Nehru like the rushed timetable?

CHRISTOPHER. He thinks it will wrong-foot Jinnah and the Muslim League. (*To* RAO.) Am I right?

RAO. I don't think Pandit-ji is that devious.

CHRISTOPHER. But you would say that.

RADCLIFFE. The adviser to my Commission he's appointed... is he a little... stiff?

CHRISTOPHER. Don't be deceived ...

RAO. No, he's formidable. Nehru wants him to be Prime Minister of Kashmir.

CHRISTOPHER. If Kashmir is to be awarded to India.

RAO. Which it must be.

CHRISTOPHER. That is for debate.

RAO. Well! We will see.

CHRISTOPHER. We will indeed.

RADCLIFFE. But I thought Nehru was charming, beautiful manners. I must own up, I thought I was going to meet some kind of nationalist fanatic.

CHRISTOPHER. Sir, be careful. Nehru is a consummate politician.

RAO. He needs to be.

CHRISTOPHER. And damn well nearly a communist.

RAO. I...

RADCLIFFE. Well, be that or no, I feel encouraged.

Enter a BRITISH ARMY SERGEANT.

Well, one witness down, one to go.

RAO. With respect, sir, your Commission is not a court.

RADCLIFFE. Oh it is, Mr Ayer. Though I don't know if I'm on the judge's bench or in the dock. There's our driver. (*To* CHRISTOPHER.) Jinnah, how do I …

CHRISTOPHER. No title, just Mister. Muhammad Ali Jinnah prides himself on being plain.

RADCLIFFE. Well. Excellent.

They exit.

Scene Eight

MUHAMMAD ALI JINNAH*'s office. Desk. Shuttered calm.*

JINNAH *– seventy-one, tall, straight-backed – is alone, standing looking out of the window, very still.*

Enter LIAQUAT ALI KHAN, *fifty-two.*

LIAQUAT. They're here.

JINNAH. Very well.

LIAQUAT. A Hindu is with them. Shall I ask for him to be excluded?

JINNAH. Who is he?

LIAQUAT. Rao V.D. Ayer.

JINNAH. Ah. So Nehru has got his spy close to the Commission.

LIAQUAT. I will insist he is excluded.

JINNAH (*dismissive wave of the hand*). No no no.

LIAQUAT. Everything will go straight back to the Congress Party.

JINNAH. Let it.

LIAQUAT. Very well.

He turns to go.

JINNAH. They can wait. The British have rushed this judge on us, we will slow him down. (*A beat.*) I can't recall a Judge Radcliffe in an Indian court.

LIAQUAT. That's because he's never been in one. Or in India at all.

JINNAH. Really? Have the British sent a fool? Do they want to turn partition into a Gilbert and Sullivan opera?

LIAQUAT. I've made enquiries. He's not a fool.

JINNAH. What is he then?

LIAQUAT. Principled.

JINNAH. An Englishman with principles, come to take a meat cleaver to the country. Allah protect us.

LIAQUAT. But from their point of view, what can they do? Since the Hindus sank negotiations last year, they've lost control.

JINNAH. We all sank the negotiations. Did any of us know what we would unleash? Did I, when I called for a Day of Action last year, and cities burnt? Hatred and suspicion on all sides, Muslim and Hindu and Sikh. Just a tinge of differences in ideology or religion works like a bomb.

LIAQUAT. But we will have Pakistan.

JINNAH. But what Pakistan? A bleeding corpse, which we'll be expected to live in like maggots?

LIAQUAT. We will not let that happen. We must bend this judge, make him see reason.

JINNAH *scoffs*.

JINNAH. When I began the struggle for Muslim rights, I never thought of India split in two.

LIAQUAT. Jinnayah, our own people have forced this upon us. There is no going back.

JINNAH. I know. I can only pray that a divided India is the will of Allah.

LIAQUAT. This melancholy. You must not give way to it.

JINNAH *does not reply. A pause.*

JINNAH. Let us see our musically comic judge, then.

LIAQUAT *exits quickly.*

JINNAH *looking out of the window. Then he looks at a newspaper on the desk.*

Eight across. (*A pause.*) Long-legged fly... seven letters...

LIAQUAT *enters with* RADCLIFFE, CHRISTOPHER *and* RAO.

LIAQUAT. Mr Radcliffe, I have the honour of introducing you to Mr Muhammad Ali Jinnah.

JINNAH. Mr Justice Radcliffe.

A handshake.

RADCLIFFE. Mr Jinnah, I am delighted to meet you. These are members of my staff: Mr Christopher Beaumont, Mr Rao Ayer.

JINNAH. Gentlemen.

Handshakes.

CHRISTOPHER. Sir.

AYER. Sir.

JINNAH *gestures to them to sit. They do.*

A silence.

JINNAH *is dead still. Suddenly he turns to* RADCLIFFE.

JINNAH. Mr Justice, let us do without flimflam and speak frankly.

RADCLIFFE. Please.

JINNAH. Why has the British Government suddenly imposed the fourteenth of August as the date of Independence?

RADCLIFFE. Respectfully, sir, I cannot speak to that, it is a decision of the British Government.

JINNAH. But you are the instrument sent to implement it.

RADCLIFFE. It is a political matter.

JINNAH. And carving up the subcontinent is not?

RADCLIFFE. Again, sir, with respect, I am the servant not the master. You must protest to the Viceroy.

JINNAH. As I have, in no uncertain terms.

RADCLIFFE. That is your right.

JINNAH. Oh, I do not know what rights Muslims have in this matter.

RADCLIFFE. The right to a fair hearing. We all wish to do the best for India.

JINNAH. Ah there, there you have it.

RADCLIFFE. I'm sorry…

JINNAH. India is not a nation, or a country. It is a subcontinent of nationalities.

RADCLIFFE. Yes, but…

JINNAH. Muslim, Hindu, Sikh, Tamil, Farsi, there are Arabs on the West Coast, there are Jews, two thousand ethnic groups, four major languages…

RADCLIFFE. I…

JINNAH. You British make this mistake, every time you colonise. You move into a huge area of the globe and call it 'a country', when it is not. You have done so all over Africa, in Arab countries, in Iraq.

RADCLIFFE. All… Mr Jinnah, all I want is a level playing field.

LIAQUAT *angry*.

LIAQUAT. Mr Justice, this is not a cricket match!

JINNAH *laughs*. LIAQUAT *laughs. Uneasy smiles from* RADCLIFFE*'s group*.

A pause.

JINNAH. Mr Justice, I have to tell you that some of my colleagues in the Muslim League think I should withdraw all cooperation with you.

RADCLIFFE. Mr Jinnah, that would be a most grave and serious step.

JINNAH. Would it not. (*A beat*.) But I do wish us to understand each other.

RADCLIFFE. As do I.

JINNAH. Cricket metaphors aside.

He looks away out of the window. He is very still.

'Where is Pakistan?' that is the question. You see, for years Muslims did not think of Pakistan as a place at all. Many still don't. Pakistan is everywhere and nowhere, a country of the heart. Some have seen the whole of the subcontinent becoming Pakistan. I myself, for years, did not want a partition, I did all I could to make a federated India, with guarantees for Muslims, in a power-sharing government. But it is not to be, the hatred has become too great. So now we actually have to make a place, on the ground, on the map. My fear is this: that we will end up with a ragged line, a moth-eaten Pakistan, where my people will not be able to live. (*A beat*.) Calcutta must be in Pakistan.

A silence.

RADCLIFFE. Mr Jinnah, with respect, I cannot discuss hard cases.

LIAQUAT. Pakistan must have a port in the east. It can only be Calcutta.

RAO. India cannot be without a port in the east, India must have Calcutta.

LIAQUAT. Pakistan will be cut off.

RAO. It is a Hindu city.

LIAQUAT. It is nearly half Muslim!

RAO. And more than half Hindu!

LIAQUAT. Then make the sacrifice! You demand we make
sacrifices! All over the Punjab!

RAO. Calcutta is Indian in spirit!

LIAQUAT. But Muslim by right!

RAO. Its temples are sacred.

LIAQUAT. What is not sacred on this earth?

RAO. It is ours!

LIAQUAT. It is ours!

RADCLIFFE. Gentlemen, please could we have some order...

LIAQUAT. Or what, Mr Justice, you will clear the court?

JINNAH. Order there must be.

RADCLIFFE. Thank you.

JINNAH. But the hatred, my dear Radcliffe, the hatred. We are
educated men in this room, but even we can barely control it.
We must have a viable Pakistan, a state in which we can live
and breathe as free human beings, which we can develop
according to our own lights and culture, an Islamic
democracy with Islamic social justice and equality on our
own native soil.

RADCLIFFE. Yes. Absolutely. And that I am determined to...
effect.

JINNAH. Well. I was told you are a man of principle.

RADCLIFFE. I hope I am.

JINNAH. So does Pakistan.

A pause.

RADCLIFFE. Well...

RADCLIFFE, CHRISTOPHER *and* RAO *stand. A moment
still then they walk away.*

JINNAH *and* LIAQUAT *remain on the stage.*

CHRISTOPHER. Where is our driver?

RAO. He will be here.

RADCLIFFE, CHRISTOPHER *and* RAO *exit*.

JINNAH, *pouring then drinking a glass of whisky*.

LIAQUAT. But how *can* we deal with a man who thinks the world is a cricket pitch?

JINNAH. Be better at cricket than he is?

They laugh.

Whisky?

LIAQUAT. No... I... no.

JINNAH. You wish I didn't drink alcohol? As 'Father of an Islamic nation'? I will just have to be forgiven, won't I. Or understood.

He drinks.

A telephone rings. LIAQUAT *answers*.

LIAQUAT. There's a disturbance.

JINNAH. Who?

LIAQUAT. RSS.

JINNAH. They are trying to attack these offices?

LIAQUAT. We have our people at the end of the street...

JINNAH. Make sure Radcliffe's party has got away safely.

LIAQUAT. Of course.

He exits quickly. JINNAH *alone. He looks out of the window again.*

JINNAH. Moves upon silence.

JINNAH puts the whisky glass down, writes the answer to the crossword clue and exits.

RADCLIFFE *and* CHRISTOPHER *are still on the stage.*

RADCLIFFE. Do you find Jinnah somewhat... prickly?

CHRISTOPHER. Yes, but impressive.

RADCLIFFE. Oh very. He got eight across.

CHRISTOPHER *looks at him.*

Yesterday's *Times* crossword. The clue was 'Italian fly hushed upon, seven letters'.

CHRISTOPHER. I see.

RADCLIFFE. The answer was 'silence'.

CHRISTOPHER *does not follow.*

It's the poem by Yeats about Julius Caesar. 'Caesar is in his tent… Like a long-legged fly upon the stream / His mind moves upon silence.' Jinnah got it.

CHRISTOPHER. Did you, sir?

RADCLIFFE. Of course.

RAO *enters quickly.*

Off: shouting and chanting. Breaking glass.

RAO. The car's waiting but there's a disturbance.

RADCLIFFE. Disturb…

RAO. We must go, now.

Enter LIAQUAT, *with two* AIDES.

LIAQUAT. Mr Justice, please, we will help… Come! Now!

Off: the roars and clashes of a riot.

CHRISTOPHER (*to* LIAQUAT). Who is it?

LIAQUAT. RSS.

RADCLIFFE. Who…

CHRISTOPHER. Hindu Nazis.

RADCLIFFE. There are Hindu Nazis?

The riot louder.

A BRITISH ARMY DRIVER *runs on. And, but for*
LIAQUAT, *they all exit, running crouched, as stones are
thrown onto the stage.*

The riot climaxes.

And later, MEN *and* WOMEN *enter with brooms and sweep
the street.*

Enter JINNAH. *Two armed* AIDES *are watchful.*

JINNAH. How many?

LIAQUAT. Thirteen dead, forty-seven injured in hospitals, as
far as we can count.

JINNAH sighs.

It could have been worse, with the presence of the British.

JINNAH. Muhammad, my friend, we are at a serious
disadvantage. The British will always favour Hindus. They
think their religion is pretty, despite the savagery of its
grotesque gods, the horrors of the caste system. But the
British see Islam as iron-grey and frightening.

LIAQUAT. We have yet to nominate the official Muslim League
adviser to Radcliffe's Commission. It has to be Din
Muhammad.

JINNAH. Yes. But give him an assistant, a firebrand. We have
enough of them.

LIAQUAT. Who do you suggest?

JINNAH. Chaudhry Muhammad Ali. He knows the Raj inside
out.

LIAQUAT. Our brightest and our best.

JINNAH. We are going to need them.

They exit.

Scene Nine

MOUNTBATTEN. *He paces, smoking.*

EDWINA *paces, smoking.*

MOUNTBATTEN. God dammit. God dammit. Be in a ship. Command. Oh to. God dammit.

EDWINA. Just be on a bloody ship then, jolly hornpipes and rogers.

MOUNTBATTEN. Oh, tosh.

EDWINA. Tosh? Well, tish.

MOUNTBATTEN. God, can't we talk to each other like human beings any more?

EDWINA. Are we human beings any more?

MOUNTBATTEN. God God God! (*A beat.*) What were we arguing about?

EDWINA. Morphine. The drug morphine.

> MOUNTBATTEN *stares at his cigarette. He looks around. A servant,* ABEER, *comes forward quickly with an ashtray.*

> MOUNTBATTEN *stubs his cigarette out.* EDWINA *stubs her cigarette out.*

MOUNTBATTEN. Thank you, Abeer.

ABEER (*bows*). Your Excellency.

EDWINA. Thank you, Abeer.

ABEER. My lady. Your Excellency, My Lady, will you require further cigarettes?

MOUNTBATTEN. No, thank you, thank you, Abeer…

EDWINA. And perhaps you could leave us for now, Abeer?

ABEER. Thank you, My Lady. (*Aside*.) I collect all their cigarette stubs, not just from these two, from the Viceroy House offices, pounds of tobacco, I give it to my younger nephew and he makes cigarettes, fake Senior Service, his cousin makes the packets, they have ten people working for them, I, of course, am given a cut, they are very good boys. And when the British go and the supply dries up... we will diversify.

He exits.

EDWINA. All I was trying to say is that morphine is running out in the Bombay camps.

MOUNTBATTEN *turns away. Then he decides.*

MOUNTBATTEN. This business will end.

EDWINA. What business?

MOUNTBATTEN. Your business.

EDWINA. You want me to end overseeing medical supplies to refugees?

MOUNTBATTEN. Don't be obtuse.

EDWINA. Oh, 'obtuse'!

MOUNTBATTEN. Yes, obtuse! Dear God, do you want me to say it out loud?

EDWINA. Why not?

MOUNTBATTEN. The man's the future Prime Minister of India.

EDWINA. Yes and won't he be wonderful at it.

A silence.

MOUNTBATTEN. End it now.

EDWINA. Dicky, don't stand there like some wronged Victorian husband, it's too ridiculous.

MOUNTBATTEN. I am telling you: end it.

EDWINA. Let's not speak of this again. If we don't speak of this again, everything will be fine.

MOUNTBATTEN. Don't you realise the harm, the mockery… they are all talking.

EDWINA. 'They'? Who is this 'they'?

MOUNTBATTEN. I have made a decision.

EDWINA. Oh dear, not again, Dicky, you're so bad at them.

MOUNTBATTEN. I am taking you out of harm's way.

EDWINA. You are doing what?

MOUNTBATTEN. You will come back to England with me immediately after the handover.

EDWINA. No. I cannot. My refugee charities, they need me.

MOUNTBATTEN. Charitable needs. (*Scoffs.*) Well, I know your need, darling. You're just hot for your darkie.

She stares at him.

EDWINA. You did not say that. I will not have you say that. You did not say that. You did not.

MOUNTBATTEN. Edwina, I… (*A beat.*) I will get you back home with me, whatever the… (*Stops.*)

EDWINA. Ever the what? (*A beat.*) Cost? (*A beat.*) Cost of what?

MOUNTBATTEN. The harm, the mockery…

EDWINA. Yes, yes, and you will stop it by… what?

A silence.

The timetable…

MOUNTBATTEN. What of it?

EDWINA. The pressure you put on Atlee to rush the Independence Bill through…

MOUNTBATTEN. It was a political assessment.

EDWINA. It was going to be in nine months. Then suddenly Downing Street brought it all forward, in a rush, and that stuffed shirt Radcliffe was foisted on us…

MOUNTBATTEN. He was not foisted.

EDWINA. He's a hatchet man. Who thinks he's an English gentleman. In God's name, Dicky, what have you done...?

MOUNTBATTEN. I gave my advice, it was seasoned.

EDWINA. Seasoned.

MOUNTBATTEN. With considerable experience.

EDWINA. Experience of, what... me?

MOUNTBATTEN. You think I'd wreck all of India, just for you?

She stares at him.

EDWINA. The Bombay camps are running out of morphine. That's all I can say. That's all...

MOUNTBATTEN. I'll find some cash from somewhere.

EDWINA. Thank you.

She turns and walks away.

MOUNTBATTEN. We're running out of it. Cash. That's the truth. Atlee wants to get out, now, right away. The truth! The British Government's damn well nearly bankrupt. We can't afford to be here any longer.

She has stopped to listen. But now she exits without saying anything.

(*Aside.*) Radcliffe, for the sake of peace, peace of mind, peace... draw the line. Right through them. Their heads, their... I don't care. Draw it.

End of Act One.

ACT TWO

Scene One

The bungalow in the grounds of Viceroy House.

The windows are barred and have shutters. Lamps. Two large ceiling fans swing their long blades. A large map of India on a wall. Smaller maps on easels. Small tables around the room laden with books and documents, clubby leather chairs beside them. A large snooker table with a board over it, covered in maps. A drinks table.

CHRISTOPHER *is sorting out small maps on the big table.*

RAO *enters, carrying thick bundles of papers.*

RAO. Is the Judge…

CHRISTOPHER. Bathroom.

RAO. Any better?

CHRISTOPHER. 'Fraid not.

RAO. How often?

CHRISTOPHER. About every twenty minutes.

RAO. That is not good.

CHRISTOPHER. No. Are they the complete census figures?

RAO. Yes. Though what use Radcliffe thinks they will be, I do not know.

CHRISTOPHER. Well, if he's going to make decisions, he needs some information.

RAO. Even though it's inaccurate?

CHRISTOPHER. Accuracy is irrelevant. I need a G and T. You?

RAO. Why not?

CHRISTOPHER *goes to the drinks table*.

What's he taking? For the… (*Gesture at his stomach*.)

CHRISTOPHER. Milk of Magnesia.

RAO. He should take essence of figs.

CHRISTOPHER. I'd say figs are the opposite of what he needs.

RAO. It's two different philosophies: 'flush right through' or 'block up'.

CHRISTOPHER. I'm a block-up man myself. God, there's ice!

RAO. No luxury spared for the fall of the British Empire.

CHRISTOPHER. Should damn well hope not.

CHRISTOPHER *is making them drinks*.

RAO. Christopher, we've wasted a week, waiting for the census figures. And we've no idea how accurate they are. And the Judge is throwing up three times an hour. This is an impossible task.

CHRISTOPHER. But we are going to do it.

RAO. How can we?

CHRISTOPHER. We have no choice.

RAO. There is always a choice.

CHRISTOPHER. You sound like Gandhi.

RAO. Christopher, we have been friends but… you know I didn't want to work for the Commission.

CHRISTOPHER. But you had orders from Nehru.

A beat.

RAO. Yes.

CHRISTOPHER. To spy for him.

RAO. As you spy for Jinnah.

A beat. CHRISTOPHER *does not reply*.

We follow our consciences.

CHRISTOPHER. On twisty paths.

RAO. Yes.

CHRISTOPHER. But whatever happens, you and I must remain friends.

RAO. We will.

CHRISTOPHER *hands him a drink and sits. They sip.*

Nehru went to see Gandhi.

CHRISTOPHER. And?

RAO. The Mahatma... is in his own world.

CHRISTOPHER. If he came out in support of the border...

RAO. He won't.

CHRISTOPHER. Is he aware of the chaos?

RAO. No doubt. But in his own way.

CHRISTOPHER. It's like he's abandoned his people, abandoned all of us.

RAO. It's religion.

CHRISTOPHER. I don't understand.

RAO. No, you don't.

CHRISTOPHER *sighs.*

CHRISTOPHER. I was in a Punjab village. Intelligent men. One had served in the war, in the Sudan. Do you know what made them lose their temper?

RAO. The price of matches?

CHRISTOPHER. You know about that?

RAO. It's happening all over the country.

CHRISTOPHER. But matches?

RAO. It's the little things.

CHRISTOPHER. That's what he said...

RAO. The little things that move the masses, and kill. (*A beat.*) The complexity of it, Christopher. How can this judge begin to grasp...

A wave of the hand.

CHRISTOPHER. He's an honourable man.

RAO. Aren't they all?

CHRISTOPHER *picks up a book on the arm of the chair and looks at it.*

CHRISTOPHER. No, this is a man with a very good brain.

He opens the book and laughs.

RAO. What?

CHRISTOPHER. Did you give him this?

RAO. No, what is it?

CHRISTOPHER. The Bhagavad Gita.

RAO. He's reading the Bhagavad Gita?

CHRISTOPHER. Give him credit. He's trying to understand India.

RAO. Oh, you 'enlightened' rulers. How you all want to 'understand India', to screw her the better.

CHRISTOPHER. You know, I could rather take exception to that.

RAO. But you won't, because you know it to be true.

CHRISTOPHER. Rao, it's up to us, in this room, with these maps. We make two new countries, or India collapses into endless bloodletting and ceases to exist.

RAO. And to achieve that London has sent us an ignorant judge?

Enter RADCLIFFE. *He has overheard.* CHRISTOPHER *and* RAO *stand.*

RADCLIFFE. Show me this place Ferozepur again, but on a bigger-scale map.

RAO. Yes, sir, it's...

RADCLIFFE. And are those the census figures?

RAO. Yes, sir...

RADCLIFFE. About time, I thought the Raj Civil Service was a gleaming, well-oiled machine?

RAO. It is a little unoiled these days.

CHRISTOPHER. It's the treason of the clerks. Some civil servants are deserting their posts, burning official records.

RADCLIFFE. Ah. Well. I was thinking, anyway, the census was done by the British in 1941?

RAO. Yes.

RADCLIFFE. In wartime...

RAO. Yes...

RADCLIFFE. So its accuracy is in question?

RAO. Yes...

RADCLIFFE. So how can we judge where Hindu, Muslim, Sikh populations are in 1947?

RAO. We have anecdotal evidence.

RADCLIFFE. Anecdotal. Perhaps it would be better to use a water-divining stick over the map: sideways vibrating for Hindu, up and down for Muslim, and what, circles for Sikh?

RAO *and* CHRISTOPHER *are both uneasy.*

We are making a new reality. Out of an old. But the old reality... I can hardly grasp what it is. (*A beat.*) Ferozepur.

RAO. Yes, sir.

RAO *swings a map up on to the table.*

RADCLIFFE. And, Christopher, get me a damn G and T too, would you?

CHRISTOPHER. Do you think...

RADCLIFFE. Oh, for God's sake, I know we've got a nanny state back home but it's not out here too, is it?

CHRISTOPHER (*laughs*). No, sir...

RADCLIFFE's finger running over the map.

RADCLIFFE. Ferozepur, ah yes. Looks a small place to cause such upset.

RAO. Upset? Three martyrs, Indian freedom fighters, came from Ferozepur. You... the British... hanged them in 1931. Their memory is eternal and they have come to represent the struggle for freedom and they will forever be in our hearts, as will their city with its lovely gardens.

RADCLIFFE. I see. (*A beat.*) Right, the census. It's the evidence we have. Now how can we...

CHRISTOPHER. I suggest we colour code on the local maps: Hindu red, Muslim green, Sikh yellow, any other religion purple...

RADCLIFFE. Excellent... my approach is to answer Mr Jinnah's question: 'Where is Pakistan?'

RAO. You mean once you answer that, you'll know where India is?

RADCLIFFE. Yes.

RAO about to protest. CHRISTOPHER cuts in. Broad gestures at the big map on the table.

CHRISTOPHER. Well, the greatest concentration of Muslims is in the west, in the Punjab, in the north in Kashmir, and in the east in Bengal.

RADCLIFFE. It's a matter of what is just. Where there is a majority of Hindus, there is India. Where there is a majority of Muslims, there is Pakistan. This may be simpler than we think.

RAO and CHRISTOPHER look at each other.

CHRISTOPHER. In the east, yes, Bengal is largely Muslim. Maybe the line could work there.

RAO. But what of Calcutta...

CHRISTOPHER. Yes, but my point is that in the Punjab...

His hand sweeps across the map on the table.

…in the Punjab the populations are jumbled up, village by village.

RADCLIFFE. Well, presumably they can continue to live side by side whether they be in India or in Pakistan.

RAO. Hindus will never live under Muslim law.

CHRISTOPHER. And the Muslim demand for a homeland cannot be stopped.

RAO. It's the blood that's been spilt. Sir, however rational and just you are, the blood will be against you.

CHRISTOPHER. People will kill for their farms and their homes.

The three of them are still, staring at the map. RADCLIFFE *breaks the moment.*

RADCLIFFE. Right. Well. All I can suggest is we try a tentative scribble.

Scene Two

JINNAH, LIAQUAT *and* CHAUDHRY MUHAMMAD ALI. JINNAH *shakes hands with* CHAUDHRY.

JINNAH. My dear Chaudhry, I am pleased you will be an adviser to the Radcliffe Commission. You will be a great help.

CHAUDHRY. *Inshallah.*

LIAQUAT. Do we have any idea what has been going on in that bungalow?

CHAUDHRY. I can find out.

LIAQUAT. You have an informant?

CHAUDHRY. Not an informant, more a friend…

LIAQUAT. You mean the Englishman, Beaumont?

CHAUDHRY. He takes a risk, talking to me. There is the British Official Secrets Act.

LIAQUAT. Risk? No doubt he revels in it. Another would-be Lawrence of Arabia homosexual. Why does the British public-school system produce so many of them?

CHAUDHRY. I've no idea. But there are not many friends of Pakistan in Viceroy House.

LIAQUAT. When is Radcliffe seeing the advisers?

CHAUDHRY. Two days' time.

LIAQUAT. Disgraceful. They should have been consulted at once.

JINNAH. Listen to me, my brothers. We are going to be passed a legacy. With partition will come many things, good and bad, and even great evil. And we must agitate for, and struggle for, and demand a liveable Pakistan. But do not forget: this is a mighty revolution. The creation of a place that is unprecedented: an Islamic democracy. And we will make this great state of Pakistan happy and prosperous, and if we will all forget our pasts, forget our hatreds, there will be no end to the progress we can make. It's time for the afternoon prayers. Come.

They exit.

Scene Three

New coloured maps, books, strewn about. A working mess.

RADCLIFFE, RAO *and* CHRISTOPHER *are exhausted.*

They each have a large children's colouring crayon.

They are staring at the map.

Then RADCLIFFE *draws a line.*

RAO. That's a railway line.

RADCLIFFE. What?

RAO. Going into Ferozepur. You've drawn the border straight along a railway line, one rail in India the other in Pakistan.

RADCLIFFE. Then we'll move the border... a hundred yards south.

He scrawls on the map.

CHRISTOPHER. Sir, we have spent three days on a section barely fifty miles long...

RADCLIFFE. But we will get it right...

RAO. There are Hindu farms north of the line, look... a string of smallholdings.

CHRISTOPHER. And there's green to the south still. Muslim holdings...

RADCLIFFE. One yellow field.

RAO. Sikh.

CHRISTOPHER *rubs his eyes. A pause.*

RADCLIFFE. Well. We'll move the line a hundred yards north of the railway...

RAO. That puts half of Ferozepur itself in India.

CHRISTOPHER. And its population is a Muslim majority. We'll drive people from the land, they'll starve.

RADCLIFFE. Then we'll send the line around farms, ditch by ditch...

RAO. Across thousands of square miles? We may as well put on blindfolds and stick pins in the map!

CHRISTOPHER. Rao...

RAO. Sir, is this wrong?

RADCLIFFE (*wagging his finger at the map*). Well, it's very knotty round that bit...

RAO. No, doing this at all, chopping India into two, is it fundamentally wrong?

RADCLIFFE. I hope in the name of God, it is not, Mr Ayer.

CHRISTOPHER. There has to be a Muslim state...

RAO. How, by tearing the face of Mother India to bits?

RADCLIFFE. Stop this, stop this now. I have been sent to do a job, I will do it. This is a time for hard heads. I must be logical.

RAO. But surely not indifferent, sir...

RADCLIFFE. Yes, indifferent! I cannot become emotional. I cannot. Dead women, children, I cannot. It. I must rest before the meeting with the advisers. I mean, I must go mightily to the lavatory. So...

CHRISTOPHER. Yes, sir.

RAO. Yes, sir.

RADCLIFFE. Don't want the maps lying around. And sit our dignitaries up on hard chairs. Old trick: keep witnesses perky.

He exits quickly.

RAO. Does he know what he's in for with this meeting?

CHRISTOPHER. What do you think?

RAO. What the Hell does it matter what I think?

They do not speak for a while as they tidy up. Then RAO *stops.*

I apologise.

CHRISTOPHER. Yes.

RAO. I lost my temper with him.

CHRISTOPHER. You did.

RAO. I just feel the division of my country is being reduced to a farce, drenched in blood.

CHRISTOPHER. You are in the one place where you can stop that happening.

RAO. Am I? I wonder. (*A beat.*) Where's the cloth?

It's underneath the table, CHRISTOPHER *gets it.*

CHRISTOPHER. Here. One two three go…

They cover the table.

So they can't see what the Judge calls our 'scribbles'.

RAO. What will happen when they do?

CHRISTOPHER *moves five hard-backed chairs into two rows.*

CHRISTOPHER. Chairs…

Looks around, then moves hard-backed chairs into a row.

Right, do you want to eat something?

RAO. Yes.

They exit.

Scene Four

The bungalow.

The stage empty for a moment. Then RADCLIFFE *enters.*

He slouches, makes it to a chair.

He sits, breathing heavily.

He picks up the Bhagavad Gita. He opens it at random and reads.

RADCLIFFE. 'The Lord Krishna said: a man does not attain freedom from the results of actions by abstaining from actions… no one, for a moment, exists without taking action.'

He thinks.

Hunh.

He flicks to another page and reads.

'Know that darkness is born from ignorance.' Oh, I think we know that, Lord Krishna, I think we do.

The telephone rings.

He gets out of the chair. He finds the telephone and lifts it.

Justice Radcliffe, how may I…

ANTONIA *enters carrying a telephone, the receiver to her ear.*

ANTONIA. Oh, Cyril, it's taken ages to get through. Darling, how are you?

RADCLIFFE. I don't think the bottled water's boiled.

ANTONIA. What?

RADCLIFFE. The bottled water.

ANTONIA. What are you talking about?

RADCLIFFE. A stiff G and T seems to settle it.

ANTONIA. Settle what? You're not ill are you?

RADCLIFFE. Bit of a rite of passage.

ANTONIA. Rite of what?

RADCLIFFE. Back passage, I should say. Ha!

ANTONIA. What?

RADCLIFFE. Nothing.

ANTONIA. You are ill, is that what you're saying?

RADCLIFFE. No no, I'm fiddle fit, spiffing, perfect.

ANTONIA. Oh, darling, you're so far away.

RADCLIFFE. Yes. I am. (*A beat.*) Antonia...

ANTONIA. Do keep your feet dry, darling. Thick wool socks. Angela Maze-Bassett said that you must keep your feet dry in India or you get some terrible kind of fungus.

RADCLIFFE. Right.

ANTONIA. Her husband lost three toes in Jaipur.

RADCLIFFE. Good, I mean... right, I... Antonia, I'm afraid it won't be possible to bring you out here.

A beat.

ANTONIA. Cyril, why, what's happened?

RADCLIFFE. It's all a bit of a panic.

ANTONIA (*a moment*). I understand.

RADCLIFFE. I'm so sorry.

ANTONIA. But you are all right?

RADCLIFFE. Yes, yes... (*Holds the receiver away from him.*) Oh God, God...

ANTONIA. I mean, I'm sure Lord Mountbatten knows what he is doing.

RADCLIFFE. The trouble is, do I know what I'm doing?

ANTONIA. Sorry, darling, what?

RADCLIFFE. Never mind…

ANTONIA. Have you met Gandhi?

> RADCLIFFE *finds it difficult to continue.*

I said have you met Gandhi?

RADCLIFFE. This line is awful.

ANTONIA. Darling…

RADCLIFFE. Darling…

ANTONIA. I'll send more socks…

> *But the line is dead.*

RADCLIFFE (*aside*). Extraordinary. To have no control over yourself. Makes you aware of your inner being, in a queasy kind of way. Oh! Here it comes again…

> *He rushes off.*

Scene Five

The stage is empty.

Then CHRISTOPHER *and* RAO *enter, ushering in* MAHAJAN, JUSTICE DIN MUHAMMAD *and his assistant* CHAUDHRY, *and the Sikh* JUSTICE TEJA SINGH.

CHRISTOPHER. Gentlemen, if you would wait a moment I will…

> *But* RADCLIFFE *enters, wearing judge's robes, with his wig in his hand. They are taken aback.*

RADCLIFFE. Yes, gentlemen, welcome.

CHRISTOPHER. God, he's wearing…

RADCLIFFE. If you'll forgive me, the heat, I won't bewig myself.

He puts his wig in a prominent position on one of the easels used for maps.

Mr Justice Mahajan, I have already had the pleasure...

MAHAJAN. Mr Justice, sir...

RADCLIFFE. And...

CHRISTOPHER. Mr Justice Din Muhammad from the Muslim League...

DIN MUHAMMAD. Mr Justice, an honour, sir...

RADCLIFFE. Likewise and...

CHRISTOPHER. And his assistant Mr Chaudhry Muhammad Ali...

RADCLIFFE. Mr Chaudhry.

CHAUDHRY. Mr Justice.

CHRISTOPHER. Mr Justice Teja Singh from the Confederation of Sikh Organisations.

RADCLIFFE. I am very pleased to meet you, Mr Justice.

TEJA SINGH. Yes, sir.

Hiatus.

RADCLIFFE. Gentlemen, please.

They sit. TEJA SINGH is on the end of the back row. Throughout the following arguments he stays seated and still, saying nothing. CHRISTOPHER and RAO sit aside.

You have been appointed to advise the Commission which I have the honour to chair. I have made some progress in determining the border, both in the Punjab and in Bengal. I cannot, at this time, give you details of what the award may be...

Unease.

That... that will be revealed on August the seventh. But I would very much appreciate your views. This task is all but beyond me. I need your understanding, I need your wisdom.

A moment's silence. Then they blaze away.

MAHAJAN. India must have a northern border, so India must have Kashmir…

DIN MUHAMMAD (*stands*). No, sir!

MAHAJAN (*stands*). If Pakistan controls Kashmir, you could allow Chinese troops to pass the Himalayas and attack…

DIN MUHAMMAD. Pakistan will be a peace-loving country…

MAHAJAN. We have no guarantee of that.

DIN MUHAMMAD. How do we know you will not attack us?

MAHAJAN. India will be a peaceful democracy. Will Pakistan?

DIN MUHAMMAD. Of course!

MAHAJAN. Can an Islamic country be a democracy?

DIN MUHAMMAD Can a country riddled with a vicious caste system be a democracy?

MAHAJAN. Insult all you want…

CHRISTOPHER. Mr Justices…

MAHAJAN. We must secure our northern border!

DIN MUHAMMAD. If Kashmir is in India, Pakistan will be cut in half, Punjab to the west, Bengal to the east…

MAHAJAN. This talk is pointless! Kashmir is an independent state, the Maharajah will decide which country he will join…

DIN MUHAMMAD. The Maharajah of Kashmir is a British puppet…

MAHAJAN. That is a slander!

DIN MUHAMMAD. You will never have Kashmir!

MAHAJAN. Kashmir is India's!

CHAUDHRY. Gentlemen, shall we be quiet!

MAHAJAN. I will not be insulted…

DIN MUHAMMAD Nor I…

CHAUDHRY. Silence! All of you!

He stands, knocking his chair over. CHRISTOPHER *and* RAO *stand.*

All stare at CHAUDHRY.

Mr Justice Radcliffe, seventy-seven per cent of the Kashmiri people are Muslim. When Pakistan comes into existence, would not the democratic thing be to put the choice to them, in a referendum?

MAHAJAN. How many times? Kashmir is independent and not in the gift of the British Government!

RADCLIFFE. But at last an idea. I will allow this. Mr Chaudhry?

CHAUDHRY. If Britain is to leave a legacy on the subcontinent, let it be democracy. So, Mr Justice, call for a referendum in Kashmir. If you do not, you will mutilate Pakistan at the moment of its birth.

RAO. The terms of the Commission are to draw a border, not to dictate political policy...

RADCLIFFE. Mr Ayer, you are right. But Mr Chaudhry, I do hear what you say. A referendum in the disputed territory of Kashmir may well be a way of drawing the border.

MAHAJAN. That is totally...

RADCLIFFE. Gentlemen, thank you, that concludes our discussion on Kashmir.

MAHAJAN. Totally...

RADCLIFFE. I will see you all in... see you again tomorrow...

MAHAJAN. Unacceptable, totally...

RADCLIFFE. Again tomorrow, when I will hear evidence on...

CHRISTOPHER *hands him a paper.*

...Bengal and the Chittagong tract.

MAHAJAN. We must have the Chittagong tract! It is the source of hydroelectric power for Calcutta.

DIN MUHAMMAD. And how is Pakistan to light itself? By firelight?

MAHAJAN. Calcutta is India's!

DIN MUHAMMAD. You will not get Calcutta!

MAHAJAN. We will! And Ferozepur!

They move to hit each other.

CHRISTOPHER. Gentlemen!

All but RADCLIFFE *freeze. He stumbles forward. He looks at them. He looks at his hands.*

Suddenly there is a big, booming voice.

VOICE. Know that darkness.

RADCLIFFE *falls to the floor.*

And they are rushing towards him.

DIN MUHAMMAD. Mr Justice, sir…

RADCLIFFE *struggles to his feet.*

RADCLIFFE. No no, but, gentlemen, if you would excuse me…

DIN MUHAMMAD. Yes of course, Mr Justice…

RADCLIFFE *exits quickly but not in a straight line.*

CHAUDHRY. If the head of the Commission were too ill to continue, that would be a very serious matter…

RAO. It's nothing. British, first time in India…

They move towards the door.

MAHAJAN. Please do give him our sincere best wishes. Is he flushing through or blocking?

CHRISTOPHER. Blocking.

MAHAJAN. Always a mistake.

RAO. Gentlemen, I will see you to your cars.

RAO, MAHAJAN, CHAUDHRY *and* DIN MUHAMMAD *exit.*

TEJA SINGH *still sits on his chair. He and* CHRISTOPHER *look at each other.*

A pause.

CHRISTOPHER. Mr Justice?

TEJA SINGH *stands and exits.*

Jesus Christ, crying aloud, God almighty alive…

He goes to the drinks cabinet.

RAO *enters.*

RAO. This is my country these buffoons are tearing to bits.

CHRISTOPHER. The second time as farce.

RAO. What?

CHRISTOPHER. History.

RAO. Oh, that bloody stuff. Pour me one.

Enter RADCLIFFE*, out of his robes.*

RADCLIFFE. Time, like water. Rushing toward the deadline. You can feel it on your skin.

CHRISTOPHER. Sir, Lord Mountbatten's personal physician…

RADCLIFFE. No, I'm fine. The Sikh adviser was impressive.

RAO. But he didn't…

RADCLIFFE. Exactly! Didn't say a word. Give him everything he wants.

RAO *laughs.* CHRISTOPHER *does not.*

By the by, what does he want?

RAO. A Sikh homeland in the Province of Sindh.

RADCLIFFE. Sind. Which we're giving to Pakistan.

CHRISTOPHER. We are.

RADCLIFFE. Well, if we are to make fair awards to all, could Sindh be divided in two? Part Muslim, part Sikh?

RAO. There…

CHRISTOPHER. Sir… No.

RADCLIFFE. One more tinderbox ready to go up, eh? So no Sikh homeland.

A silence.

Wasn't Kashmir once ruled by the Sikhs? See: doing my reading…

CHRISTOPHER. They went to war with us in 1846. We got rid of the Sikh Prince and gave it to a pro-British Muslim.

RADCLIFFE. Scar tissue. Left by the Empire. Dangerous, scar tissue in the sun. Can flare up. Remember a holiday in Dartmouth. My appendix scar.

A distant look from RADCLIFFE.

CHRISTOPHER. Sir, about Kashmir…

RADCLIFFE. Those men are justices! Judges! How can they behave so badly?

RAO. They have no choice. Their positions are set.

RADCLIFFE. But how can they hope to create a border together?

RAO. They have no intention of creating a border! They want you to do it.

RADCLIFFE. What? So Nehru and Jinnah can blame me for anything they don't like?

He is right. RAO *and* CHRISTOPHER *look at him.*

I am, what I believe American gangsters call, 'the patsy'?

RAO. Sir…

RADCLIFFE. Right! I am cutting the advisers out. And I want to consider a referendum in Kashmir.

CHRISTOPHER. That would be disastrous. Thousands would die at the polling stations.

RADCLIFFE. I begin to suspect thousands are going to die anyway. Get me the Kashmir census figures.

CHRISTOPHER. I must protest...

RADCLIFFE. Do what you damn well want! But this is what is called the jolly old white man's burden, no? No? Which you're an expert in banging on about? So! I bear it. I decide.

He glares at them, then turns away and stumbles. They move toward him but he holds up a hand. They stop.

RADCLIFFE *steadies himself against the table and exits.*

RAO. We have a problem.

CHRISTOPHER. Yes.

Scene Six

Bungalow. RADCLIFFE, MOUNTBATTEN.

MOUNTBATTEN. So, Radcliffe, thought I'd come down, have a word. How are we doing? Sunlit uplands visible?

RADCLIFFE. The advisers from Congress and the Muslim League are impossible.

MOUNTBATTEN. Rowdy lot?

RADCLIFFE. I've cut them out of crucial discussions.

MOUNTBATTEN. Tricky. They were appointed to make the show look balanced.

RADCLIFFE. The politics of it are not my concern.

MOUNTBATTEN. No, of course not.

RADCLIFFE. I am attempting a rational, fair solution.

MOUNTBATTEN. That is what you were asked to do.

RADCLIFFE. I...

MOUNTBATTEN (*interrupts*). Hope it's not too hot here in the bungalow. Only fans down here, I know, we did consider American air-conditioning units but the cost… and since we're leaving anyway. Anything else? The tummy upset…?

RADCLIFFE. Nothing. Bad karma.

MOUNTBATTEN. Well, I have been a little concerned. But all is well, despite uppity commissioners? Good to know. Well. Think we both should get some shut-eye, don't you?

RADCLIFFE. Viceroy, the truth is that I am finding the task… Dear God, where to begin. There is Kashmir.

MOUNTBATTEN. Well…

RADCLIFFE (*interrupts*).…And there is the nightmare of the border through the Punjab, village by village, separating out the Muslim majority, the Hindu majority.

MOUNTBATTEN *is increasingly irritated.* RADCLIFFE *is animated.*

MOUNTBATTEN. Rad…

RADCLIFFE. And the Sikhs! Ignored by the Raj over the years, beaten up, villages burnt. It's all… push and shove, claim against claim.

MOUNTBATTEN. This is not…

RADCLIFFE.…to be frank, Viceroy! I cannot see my way through. Take Calcutta…

MOUNTBATTEN.…If only someone would…

RADCLIFFE.…morally, justly, Calcutta should be in Pakistan but…

MOUNTBATTEN. Just shut up will you! Shut up!

A pause. They are staring at each other.

Radcliffe, I cannot discuss any details of the award.

RADCLIFFE. I need your guidance…

MOUNTBATTEN. You cannot have it.

RADCLIFFE. But you represent the British Government.

MOUNTBATTEN. I do not. I represent the King and India is His Majesty's Imperial possession – for the next few weeks, anyway. The Crown must be above the fray. As must I.

RADCLIFFE. So it is down to me.

MOUNTBATTEN. Yes.

RADCLIFFE. Where Pakistan is to exist on the surface of the planet is down to me.

For a moment there is a flicker of indecision from MOUNTBATTEN.

MOUNTBATTEN. Yes.

RADCLIFFE. And I take the blame.

MOUNTBATTEN. Aren't judges used to being blamed?

RADCLIFFE. From people they send to prison. Am I sending a whole nation to prison?

MOUNTBATTEN. I don't think the people of India will think that.

RADCLIFFE. But what will the people of Pakistan think? Am I giving them a prison? Not a house where they can live, be free…?

MOUNTBATTEN. I'm sure what you do will be for the best.

A beat.

RADCLIFFE. Have you read the Bhagavad Gita?

MOUNTBATTEN. The Hindu religious thingy? God no.

RADCLIFFE. The warrior Arjuna is on a battlefield. He wearies at the bloodshed and refuses to fight. The god Krishna appears and tells him he has no choice. It is his karma to fight.

MOUNTBATTEN. And what does that tell you?

RADCLIFFE. Bugger all, Viceroy. Bugger all.

RADCLIFFE turns angrily and exits.

MOUNTBATTEN. In the name of holy Mother Riley, I…

He storms to a drinks table, pours himself a large whisky, then exits.

Scene Seven

Bungalow.

CHRISTOPHER *and* RAO *are working on the big table, small maps in hand, census rolls.*

RADCLIFFE, *looking haggard, storms in.*

RADCLIFFE. Where are we?

CHRISTOPHER. Calcutta.

RADCLIFFE. Right!

> *He picks up a crayon and slashes at the map.*

> There! Once and for all, Calcutta is in Pakistan. How does that look, pretty good, eh?

RAO. But India must have a port on the north-east coast.

> RADCLIFFE *points.*

RADCLIFFE. It has Madras.

RAO. A thousand miles south.

RADCLIFFE. Pakistan must have a port.

RAO. There's Chittagong.

CHRISTOPHER. But nowhere near as deep as Calcutta.

RADCLIFFE. No. Chittagong can go to India.

RAO. Sir, that is absolutely impossible! Indian goods would have to pass over the Chittagong Hills. Which obviously must be part of Pakistan.

CHRISTOPHER. Calcutta is full of Muslims.

RAO. They will live in India.

CHRISTOPHER. Or be forced to leave?

RADCLIFFE *slams his hands on the map. Then he lowers his face to it and presses his forehead down.*

CHRISTOPHER *and* RAO *do not know what to do.*

Then RADCLIFFE *straightens.*

RADCLIFFE. Very well.

He erases the line with a rubber then takes up the crayon and draws a new line.

Calcutta is in India. How many did I just kill?

He slams the crayon down on the table, splintering it.

CHRISTOPHER. I must protest!

RAO. Sir, you will be forever in the people of India's debt…

CHRISTOPHER.…You are crippling Pakistan!

RADCLIFFE. No, no more. I bear, I decide. Now go.

They do not.

I said go!

They exit.

I'm from England, little England, little… fields. Gardens. Leicester Square. What am I doing here?

He leans his head back. The telephone rings. He does not move. It rings on…

Enter ANTONIA, *holding the stick telephone.*

RADCLIFFE *does not reply. He remains slumped in his chair throughout the next scene.*

ANTONIA *gives up and puts the phone down. She pulls on a coat, puts on a hat and walks into…*

Scene Eight

Palace of Westminster. ATLEE, PETHICK-LAWRENCE *and* ANTONIA.

ATLEE. Socks.

ANTONIA. I sent them, but he never mentioned receiving them.

ATLEE. Right.

PETHICK-LAWRENCE. Thick wool socks? Yes, dry feet, the wool guards against fungus.

ATLEE. Really?

ANTONIA. And now he won't reply when I telephone. Though the operator at Viceroy House says he's there.

ATLEE. You're concerned.

ANTONIA. Yes. I'm afraid I am. Terribly.

ATLEE. Well, let me reassure you, Cyril is doing an excellent job.

ANTONIA. I fear he's… out of his depth.

ATLEE. Antonia, I'll be frank. We're decolonising a subcontinent and we are all out of our depth.

ANTONIA. It's his health. (*Lower.*) His mind.

PETHICK-LAWRENCE. Oh, I don't think…

ATLEE. Absolutely not.

PETHICK-LAWRENCE. Your husband has a mind like granite.

ATLEE. Clockwork.

ANTONIA. Granite, clockwork? I don't think I recognise him in that at all. He's really… (*Near tears.*) Oh, what can I say?

PETHICK-LAWRENCE. I know the subcontinent, the climate can make one a little… tropical. But nothing to affect a mind like Cyril's.

ATLEE. I'll ask Lord Mountbatten to let his doctor have a word.

ANTONIA. Oh, would you? I'd be so grateful.

ATLEE. Cyril is doing a very great service to the country. You must be proud.

ANTONIA. I am. Yes. Thank you so much, Prime Minister. (*Shakes hand.*) Lord Pethick-Lawrence.

PETHICK-LAWRENCE. Fred, please. And do telephone me personally at any time, I do know India.

ANTONIA. Thank you. Good afternoon.

ATLEE. Good afternoon, Antonia…

PETHICK-LAWRENCE. …Mrs Radcliffe.

She exits.

They are silent for a moment.

ATLEE. Has Mountbatten said anything?

PETHICK-LAWRENCE. Oh, Dicky swears everything's fine and dandy.

ATLEE. Wants to get his wife away from Nehru.

PETHICK-LAWRENCE. Absolutely.

ATLEE. Nehru's a good socialist.

PETHICK-LAWRENCE. Bit of a cocksman, though.

ATLEE. Politics affects some men that way. Never understood why, myself.

Pipe into mouth.

PETHICK-LAWRENCE. Clem, what if Radcliffe really is unravelling?

ATLEE. He's a professional man.

PETHICK-LAWRENCE. But if he goes potty, the damage he could do…

ATLEE. There's going to be damage anyway.

PETHICK-LAWRENCE. Maybe I should go out there, take over the reins…

ATLEE. No, Fred. This India business could end up costing the Treasury our reserves. Best thing you can do is save the airfare.

PETHICK-LAWRENCE. We do have a responsibility...

ATLEE is suddenly heated.

ATLEE. All that matters is that... that the colonisation of India ends, we lift the yoke of Imperialism from that great civilisation, that is our duty as socialists and of course it will be bloody and a mess. (*A beat.*) Let Radcliffe draw away.

They exit.

Scene Nine

The bungalow.

RADCLIFFE is still slumped in the chair. Suddenly he springs to his feet, goes to the table. He finds a pen and paper and begins to write feverishly.

RADCLIFFE (*says*). Dear Viceroy, it is my duty to tell you that I can no longer continue...

Writes. Stops.

I have found this task impossible.

Writes. Stops.

Leave India to her own devices. Therefore I tender my resignation.

Writes. Stops. Puts the pen down.

Yes. Resign.

He goes back to the chair and falls into it, face to one side.

My Lord Krishna, my limbs grow heavy, my body trembles, my mind is reeling.

The LORD KRISHNA *appears. He is young, his skin is blue. Light streams behind him.*

KRISHNA. Only by repeated practice can the mind be held steady.

RADCLIFFE. Lord, I see evil omens, nothing good can come from this, only slaughter.

KRISHNA. You have no choice.

RADCLIFFE. I have no desire to get people killed...

KRISHNA. Where do you get this weakness from? It leads only to disgrace.

RADCLIFFE. But my mind is bewildered as to what is right.

KRISHNA. Learn what impels a man to do evil. The world is enveloped by desire, by anger, as a fire is covered by smoke, as mirror by dust.

RADCLIFFE. Then I'll leave this battlefield.

KRISHNA. You cannot. A man...

RADCLIFFE/KRISHNA....A man does not attain freedom from the results of actions by abstaining from actions... for no one, even for a moment...

RADCLIFFE (*solo*)....exists without taking action.

KRISHNA. So act, invader, oppressor of my people. Do your worst. That is your nature.

KRISHNA *disappears.*

RADCLIFFE *sits up, stands up and goes to the resignation letter. He tears it up. He takes a crayon and pores over the map on the table.*

RADCLIFFE. Ferozepur! Ferozepur!

He draws.

Enter CHRISTOPHER *and* RAO.

Ah, gentlemen! I have solved the final problem of the Punjab border.

They rush to the table and stare at the map.

CHRISTOPHER. Congratulations, sir.

He and RADCLIFFE *shake hands.*

RAO. That cannot be. Ferozepur is in Pakistan.

RADCLIFFE. Action taken!

RAO. Sir, I beg you, why?

RADCLIFFE. Divine revelation.

RAO and CHRISTOPHER *exit.* RADCLIFFE *drains a whisky glass then exits.*

Scene Ten

Night meetings and conspiracies.

JINNAH, LIAQUAT *and* CHAUDHRY.

CHAUDHRY. He is favouring the Hindus, no doubt.

JINNAH. How do you know that?

CHAUDHRY. From our British friend. Radcliffe made this map this afternoon. His final decision.

He hands one of the maps used for drafting to JINNAH *and* LIAQUAT. *They open it eagerly.*

LIAQUAT. Scribbles all over the place…?

CHAUDHRY. But see the blue crayon…

LIAQUAT. What blue crayon…

CHAUDHRY. This line…

LIAQUAT. Ah. Yes, I see…

CHAUDHRY. It's the line for the division of the Punjab.

LIAQUAT. But this puts Ferozepur and hundreds of square miles in India.

JINNAH. That cannot be. It is bad to lose Calcutta, but this… It will cause terrible strife. I must see Mountbatten. (*To* CHAUDHRY.) Telephone Viceroy House.

CHAUDHRY *exits quickly.*

LIAQUAT. You cannot see Mountbatten.

JINNAH. I must confront the British!

LIAQUAT. You cannot be seen to fail.

JINNAH. I will not fail!

LIAQUAT. You cannot be seen to be snubbed by the Viceroy. If necessary, I will go.

JINNAH. This is what colonial powers do: put us into impossible situations. Suddenly, out of nowhere, comes another another impossible, irreconcilable situation. And we, the oppressed, the occupied, are made to look unreasoning, and when we protest we are called extremists, religious fanatics, terrorists. So we try to reason, to agree, and we back away. And bit by bit, we are diminished. And another nail in the lid of the coffin of our dreams is hammered home.

LIAQUAT. Jinnahnaya, we are nearly there, we nearly have our country.

JINNAH. But what will it be?

He hits the map.

A map of holes and rags? My fear is we are going to have to fight.

CHAUDHRY *enters with* CHRISTOPHER.

CHAUDHRY. Radcliffe has changed his mind. Late tonight. He's redrawn the Punjab boundary.

LIAQUAT. What, again?

CHRISTOPHER. Yes but he swears this is his final decision.

LIAQUAT. Final, final decision?

CHRISTOPHER. This time, yes. See what he's done… The border now follows this shallow depression then rises…

LIAQUAT. Ferozepur is now in Pakistan!

JINNAH. Allahu Akbar!

LIAQUAT. Allahu Akbar!

CHAUDHRY. Allahu Akbar!

> CHRISTOPHER *takes the map and they all exit quickly, looking at it.*

> *Enter* NEHRU *and* RAO.

NEHRU. Ferozepur? In Pakistan?

RAO. He changed the line again.

NEHRU. Is this certain?

RAO. He did it suddenly, late tonight.

NEHRU. What are we dealing with? A child with a box of crayons?

RAO. The terrible thing is, the terrible thing… I really do believe he is trying to be fair.

> *They look at each other, at a loss. A pause.*

NEHRU. Leave this with me, Rao.

RAO. I thought I'd tell you directly, I don't trust the telephones any more…

NEHRU. No, you did right. But be careful, next time come to my house. Goodnight.

RAO. Goodnight, Mr General Secretary.

> *Exit* RAO.

> NEHRU *crosses the stage.*

> *Enter* EDWINA. *They embrace and kiss.*

EDWINA. Jawaharlal, is this place safe?

NEHRU. Almost certainly not.

EDWINA. What is it? What's the matter?

NEHRU. Edwina, I swore to myself, when we… (*Hesitates.*)

EDWINA. When we... 'hooked up'?

NEHRU. I want you to do something, I'm so sorry to have to ask it.

EDWINA. My darling, whatever it is, I will do it.

She touches his face.

Exit NEHRU.

EDWINA *stays on the stage...*

Scene Eleven

Enter MOUNTBATTEN. *He is in full dress uniform.*

MOUNTBATTEN. We were to dine with three Maharajahs. I have dined with three Maharajahs. But my wife has not.

EDWINA. I have to talk to you.

MOUNTBATTEN. You disappeared. Without a word. Nowhere to be found.

EDWINA. We have to talk.

MOUNTBATTEN. And when I ask for the driver's log, will it be a hotel? The man's house?

EDWINA. Ferozepur cannot go to Pakistan.

MOUNTBATTEN. Oh! Is that a message from your darkie?

EDWINA. You know it cannot.

MOUNTBATTEN. The Commission has done its work, all is settled.

EDWINA. The Hindus must have Ferozepur.

MOUNTBATTEN. Do you know, I think I'm beyond bloody caring what wog gets what bit of wog land.

EDWINA. Dicky, wash your mouth out!

MOUNTBATTEN. I will not wash my mouth out!

EDWINA. You can't talk like that!

MOUNTBATTEN. I will talk how I like! Sometimes I think:
dig a bloody great ditch across the country and throw them
all in it, Hindus Muslims Sikhs and let them... Get out of the
mess as best they can.

EDWINA. Aren't we doing that anyway? Throwing them away
into a... a mass grave we've dug?

MOUNTBATTEN. Edwina, you must stop running errands for
the man, you must not, just... Stop it.

EDWINA. Oh, I don't think so. I've gone too far to 'stop it'.

MOUNTBATTEN. Have you now. Do you love him?

They stare at each other. A pause.

I would do it.

EDWINA. Do what?

MOUNTBATTEN. Wreck a continent to keep you.

EDWINA. Say any more and you and I won't survive this.

MOUNTBATTEN. The...

A pause.

The granting of Indian Independence. What I wanted to be
remembered for, one great thing. God knows I'd had balls-
ups in the past. I know in the Navy they called me the Master
of Disaster.

EDWINA. Darling...

MOUNTBATTEN. Honour. To do this, after all the mess of
Britain in India, two centuries or more of it, to leave with
honour. And I am wrecking, rushing things through just to
have a hope of keeping you...

EDWINA. If we were to go in three months time, or six
months, or next year... it would be no better. You are an
honourable man, Dicky.

MOUNTBATTEN. Doesn't count though, does it.

EDWINA. Honour always counts.

She goes to him and strokes his hair.

MOUNTBATTEN. Too late for us, is it, old girl?

She touches his face. A moment. Then she exits.

He finishes his drink. He is still for a moment, thinking. Then he exits.

Scene Twelve

Viceroy House.

MOUNTBATTEN. Radcliffe, sorry to summon you up to Viceroy House out of the blue, but...

RADCLIFFE. Lordly power.

MOUNTBATTEN. What?

RADCLIFFE. It's your Lordly power. Arjuna on the battlefield, summoned by the Lord.

MOUNTBATTEN. What are you talking about?

RADCLIFFE. Krishna. Quite a joker, isn't he.

MOUNTBATTEN. For God's sake, pull yourself together, man.

RADCLIFFE. Oh, I am pulled.

A pause.

MOUNTBATTEN. I want you to understand the situation. In seven days Nehru will be Prime Minister of India.

RADCLIFFE. I cannot change the line on Nehru's say-so.

MOUNTBATTEN. I am telling you that you must.

RADCLIFFE. You said you were neutral.

MOUNTBATTEN. Of course I'm not bloody neutral, I'm Viceroy. And I rule this country for the next few days, so... redraw the line in the Punjab!

RADCLIFFE. I have redrawn and redrawn to the point of... what is there is there, I can do no more.

MOUNTBATTEN. Radcliffe, of the two nations India will be the most populous, the most powerful. If we must favour her, so be it.

RADCLIFFE. That's realpolitik!

MOUNTBATTEN. It's all realpolitik, man!

RADCLIFFE. I must be fair!

MOUNTBATTEN. Surely you realised from the start, talk of fairness was just an outward show.

RADCLIFFE. Dear God.

A pause.

MOUNTBATTEN. I really didn't want it to come to this. I never thought it would, with you.

RADCLIFFE. Why, was I the soft touch? Ignorant? The blank canvas for you to piss all over?

MOUNTBATTEN *looks away, embarrassed.*

I cannot do this. In all conscience. I will denounce the award. Let the Indians draw the line, make or destroy their country, it's theirs after all, it's always been theirs!

MOUNTBATTEN. Don't raise your voice to me, you silly fool!

A pause.

I speak for your King. As Viceroy in this country I am your King. Are you going against your Sovereign? You have no choice. You know you don't. 'The wise should act, intent on maintaining the world.'

RADCLIFFE. What?

MOUNTBATTEN. What?

RADCLIFFE. You quoted the Bhagavad Gita.

MOUNTBATTEN. Did I?

A pause.

RADCLIFFE. I'll redraw the line, back to the previous position we settled on. (*Clicks fingers.*) There... Ferozepur is India's.

He sags.

MOUNTBATTEN. It was always an impossible job, Radcliffe. You have done it extremely well. (*A beat.*) And I can tell you that the Cabinet Office have accepted my recommendation you be knighted for this great service to the Empire.

RADCLIFFE. I will not be accepting my fee.

MOUNTBATTEN. Oh. I thought five thousand pounds generous. But I'm sure it could be increased...

RADCLIFFE. I mean, I will not take any money for what I have done.

MOUNTBATTEN. In Hell's name, why not?

RADCLIFFE. I am ashamed. And I will not accept a knighthood.

MOUNTBATTEN. Oh, that you damn well will. If you snub a knighthood it'll be obvious you disapprove of the border. That would be terribly damaging, here and at home. You take the KG.

RADCLIFFE. Keep the outward show.

MOUNTBATTEN. Spruce yourself up, man. And... bloody well done. Yes.

He exits.

RADCLIFFE *alone.*

RADCLIFFE. Maintain the world.

Scene Thirteen

Enter RAO *and* CHRISTOPHER.

CHRISTOPHER. He won't see me.

RAO. Wait.

A young woman, KALVATI, *who is with* GANDHI, *enters.*

KALVATI. He is coming out to see you.

Enter GANDHI. *He carries a low folding stool. He opens it and sits.* KALVATI *leads* RAO *and* CHRISTOPHER *to him and they greet him with great respect.*

RAO. Namaste, Gandhi-ji.

CHRISTOPHER. Namaste, Gandhi-ji.

RAO. Thank you for seeing us.

GANDHI. No no, you are in plain sight. (*Laughs.*) Would you like some goats' yogurt?

RAO. Yes…

CHRISTOPHER. Yes…

GANDHI. Kalvati, my dear, for our guests?

KALVATI. Yes, Gandhi-ji.

She exits.

GANDHI. She is from Kashmir.

GANDHI *looks at* CHRISTOPHER, *waiting.*

CHRISTOPHER. The Commission has failed over Kashmir.

GANDHI. No, you have left Hindu and Muslim to fight it out. And they will.

CHRISTOPHER. Gandhi-ji…

GANDHI. Are you in despair, Mr Beaumont? Is that why you asked Rao to persuade me to see you?

CHRISTOPHER. I...

GANDHI. You think I have some kind of magic? That even now on the very eve of partition, if I gave my blessing to the border you have cut across India's breast and belly, lives would be saved?

CHRISTOPHER. Yes.

GANDHI. My dear boy, I cannot give blessings.

CHRISTOPHER. You are a religious man.

GANDHI. Am I? Oh dear me. The one thing I know about God is that he has no religion.

CHRISTOPHER. What is your counsel then, despair?

GANDHI. I do despair at times, who does not? But when I do, I remember that all through history the way of love and truth has always won. There have been tyrants and murderers, and for a time they can seem invincible, but in the end, they always fall. Think of it. Always, they fall. As the British have in India.

CHRISTOPHER. This is claptrap!

His temper lost, stands.

RAO. Christopher!

CHRISTOPHER. We have given you liberty and democracy!

GANDHI. What difference does it make to the dead, the orphans and the homeless, whether mad destruction is wrought under the name of totalitarianism or liberty and democracy?

CHRISTOPHER. What is it? You want to keep pure? Is that why you will not intervene? Why you would not see Judge Radcliffe?

GANDHI (*calm*). I will not let anyone walk through my mind with their dirty feet.

CHRISTOPHER. I cannot understand you.

GANDHI. That is because you want to be forgiven.

A moment, then CHRISTOPHER *storms away, nearly bumping into* KALVATI, *who has entered with two glasses of yogurt. He exits.*

Go after him, Rao, go after your friend.

RAO. No, Gandhi-ji, I think not.

GANDHI. It is bitter, when friendship is broken.

RAO. I know where I belong.

GANDHI. Well, in that, at least, you and I are fortunate. (*Standing with* RAO's *help*.) Come into the house and drink the yogurt with me. I did not want Mr Beaumont to be inside my house.

They exit.

Scene Fourteen

NEHRU *and* EDWINA, *making a stately progress through a refugee camp. They clasp their hands and bow right and left.*

Two WOMEN *rush forward. The first to speak has a baby.*

FIRST WOMAN. Pandit Nehru, you are a bastard!

SECOND WOMAN. Nehru, may your soul rot for ever!

NEHRU *and* EDWINA *recoil.*

NEHRU. My sisters, what…

EDWINA, *sensing the danger, pulls him by his arm.*

EDWINA. Jawarharlal, no…

FIRST WOMAN. Lady, my daughter, she has no home, it was in Lahore, now it is this terrible place…

SECOND WOMAN. Bring my mother back! Bring my sisters back!

NEHRU. Please understand, your struggle is mine...

SECOND WOMAN. My mother and my sisters are dead!

The FIRST WOMAN *holds the baby out.*

FIRST WOMAN. Please please!

For a moment they are still, staring at each other.

NEHRU. I know the suffering, but we have a new country, it is so hard, but we must...

And the SECOND WOMAN *hits* NEHRU *hard on the face.*

All dead still, shocked. Then the two WOMEN *run away and exit.*

NEHRU *and* EDWINA t*urn away.*

Scene Fifteen

NEHRU *and* EDWINA, *a private room.*

NEHRU. They turn on me. After all the years of struggle, my own people turn on me.

EDWINA. It was an isolated incident, the poor woman was distressed... one woman...

NEHRU. No, no, you know that's not true, the hostility towards us in the camp. They wanted to kill me! Kill you! The stones... My darling, your arm...

EDWINA. It's nothing.

NEHRU. I will get medical attention.

EDWINA. You will do nothing of the sort.

NEHRU. Don't they realise how much you care?

EDWINA. If I were one of them, I would throw stones.

NEHRU. No, you would not.

EDWINA. That woman who held out her baby, did she want me to take it?

NEHRU (*he is very tired*). I don't know, I don't know.

EDWINA. What can we do for them?

NEHRU. Only one thing. Look to the future.

EDWINA. No, for the people in the camps, what can we do now?

NEHRU *pauses*.

NEHRU. When the Punjab is divided, the migration will become a flood. Muslims will go north, Hindus will come south. There will be hundreds of thousands of refugees in Delhi. We plan to set up tents in the parks. Some kind of system for families who have been split up to find each other. That is what we will do.

EDWINA. I've been a fool, dreaming of happiness...

NEHRU. We will be happy! Out of the chaos we will have a free India. It will be the largest democracy on earth.

EDWINA. Oh, Mr Statesman, I meant happiness for you and me.

NEHRU. Ah. How that would be possible, I do not know.

EDWINA. I divorce Dicky and marry you.

NEHRU. Love on the world's stage?

EDWINA. Yes! You're making a new world, why shouldn't we be new in it?

NEHRU *laughs*.

NEHRU. It would make a splash.

EDWINA. Yes.

NEHRU. I'd send the Indian Navy to claim you.

EDWINA. Please do.

NEHRU. Send it up the River Thames. Fire a broadside at Buckingham Palace.

EDWINA. I'm not playing. I want to be your wife.

A silence.

I do.

NEHRU *smiles.*

NEHRU. The First Lady of India.

She is near tears.

EDWINA. Oh God.

NEHRU. You would be wonderful. You would be the mother of the country.

EDWINA. This is our last time together, isn't it?

NEHRU. Yes. We're not like other people, you see. We are world leaders. We can never turn away, be ourselves.

EDWINA. They'll make Dicky an Earl, you know, I'll be a Countess.

NEHRU. It will become you.

EDWINA. Oh God, I can't...

NEHRU. You can. We both can. But I will always adore you.

EDWINA *exits.* NEHRU *stays on the stage.*

Scene Sixteen

Enter JINNAH *and* GANDHI. *They speak aside.*

As they speak, RADCLIFFE *enters. In British clothes. He is burning papers in a brazier in his Oxford garden.*

NEHRU. Long years ago we made a tryst with destiny...

JINNAH. It is with feelings of greatest happiness and emotion that I send you my greetings...

NEHRU....and now the time comes when we shall redeem our pledge, not wholly or in full measure, but very substantially...

JINNAH. The creation of the new state has placed a tremendous responsibility on the citizens of Pakistan...

NEHRU....At the stroke of the midnight hour, when the world sleeps, India will awake to life and freedom...

JINNAH....It gives us an opportunity to demonstrate to the world how a nation, containing many elements, can live in peace and amity and work for the betterment of all its citizens, irrespective of caste or creed...

NEHRU....A moment comes, which comes but rarely in history, when we step out from the old to the new, when an age ends, and when the soul of a nation, long suppressed, finds utterance.

JINNAH....This day marks the end of a poignant phase in our national history and it should also be the beginning of a new and a noble era. We have no ambition beyond the desire to live honourably and let others live honourably...

GANDHI. Hindus should never be angry against the Muslims. If they put all of us to the sword, we should court death bravely. Offer yourselves as non-violent willing sacrifices. We are all destined to be born and die, then why need we feel gloomy over it?

The leaders remain.

Enter ANTONIA. *She carries an unopened umbrella.*

ANTONIA. Darling, it's coming on to rain, what are you doing?

RADCLIFFE. Burning it all, the papers, all the maps...

ANTONIA. Cyril, my dear, it's settled, it's done.

RADCLIFFE. You think so?

They look at the fire for a moment. Then ANTONIA *looks up and is opening her umbrella.*

End of play.